Detectives of the Sky

Investigating Aviation Tragedies

by Michael Dorman

Every time an airplane crashes, there is a mystery to be solved. What caused the crash? Engine failure, pilot error, structural defects, sabotage—the range of possibilities is enormous. An elite corps of federal investigators, known unofficially as the "detectives of the sky," is on around-the-clock call to do the job. Immediately following an air accident, the investigators rush to the crash site to begin looking for telltale clues.

Even though statistics indicate that a person is 24 times more likely to be killed in an automobile than an airliner, there is always room for improvement in our aviation safety record. The "detectives of the sky" work for the National Transportation Safety Board and are responsible for investigating every important plane crash in the United States and those abroad involving U.S. aircraft. The investigators are dedicated specialists in numerous fields relating to the construction and operation of aircraft. Combining old-fashioned in-

(Continued on back flap)

Detectives of the Sky

Detectives of the Sky

Investigating Aviation Tragedies

by Michael Dorman

FRANKLIN WATTS | NEW YORK | LONDON | 1976

Photographs courtesy of: United Press International: 17, 19, 42, 78, 79; National Transportation Safety Board: 3, 5, 56; Wide World Photos: 33, 44.

Library of Congress Cataloging in Publication Data

Dorman, Michael.
  Detectives of the Sky.

  Bibliography: p.
  Includes index.
  SUMMARY: Describes the work of government investigators of airplane crashes, citing types of accidents and specific crashes.
    1.   Aeronautics—Accident investigation—Juvenile literature. [1. Aeronautics—Accident investigation] I. Title.
TL553.5.D65   363.2'3   76–14858
ISBN 0–531–00342–6

For my aviator brother-in-law, Stuart A. O'Brien,
with the hope that his skies stay clear and safe

Contents

Detectives of the Sky

An explosion shatters an airliner flying over Colorado. The plane plunges to earth, and everyone aboard is killed. What caused the explosion? Could it have been a bomb?

Two huge airliners collide over New York City, raining debris on the metropolis and killing 136 persons—all those on both planes and 8 on the ground below. How could such a collision occur? And what could be done to prevent others in the future?

A Turkish jumbo jet, built in the United States, crashes near Paris with heavy loss of life. Investigation discloses that the tragedy could have been averted if safety recommendations made following a previous crash had been heeded. What could be done to ensure stricter enforcement of safety standards and prevent bureaucratic inefficiency from endangering the lives of those who travel by air?

These incidents and the questions they raise focus attention on the vital work of an elite group of investigators known unofficially as the "detectives of the sky." The investigators work for an agency of the United States government called the National Transportation Safety Board (NTSB). They are responsible for investigating every important plane crash in the United States and those abroad involving aircraft built or headquartered here. The NTSB investigators—experts in numerous fields relating to construction and operation of aircraft—discover the probable causes of all but a tiny fraction of the

accidents. They then make recommendations aimed at averting similar crashes in the future. As will be seen, however, their recommendations are not always pursued. Sometimes there are tragic consequences. Other government agencies, airlines, manufacturers, labor unions representing flight-crew members, and other segments of the aviation community have long resisted NTSB suggestions, out of a variety of motives. At this writing, Congress is considering legislation to provide tougher safety-enforcement measures—which are long overdue.

To perform the specialized work required, the NTSB has assembled a new breed of detectives who combine old-fashioned investigative skills with the latest in pilot training and scientific techniques. All are required to hold commercial pilots' licenses; many have spent years flying for airlines or military services. But, in addition, they must possess special engineering or technical skills in diverse fields such as metallurgy, propulsion, and meteorology.

The NTSB Bureau of Aviation Safety, headed by a veteran detective of the sky, Charles O. Miller, has only one hundred investigators. Most are assigned to the bureau's Washington headquarters, but some operate from field offices across the country. A group of ten investigators called a "go team" is on around-the-clock alert to rush to the scene of any major plane crash. Assignments to the team are rotated among the investigators. When they are on call for the team, they are required—no matter where they go —to wear an automatic paging device that gives off a beeping noise to alert them to call their office on demand. They must keep a suitcase packed at all times, and be prepared to become airborne en route to a crash scene within ninety minutes of receiving travel orders. A government jet is kept on twenty-four-hour standby at Washington National Airport for use by the go team.

Investigators survey the wreckage of a TWA Convair 880 that crashed near Cincinnati on November 20, 1967.

On arrival at the scene, each team member organizes and heads a group of investigators assigned to inquire into one of the ten general subject areas that usually provide clues to the cause of the crash. Members of these groups are not all NTSB investigators. Some have been placed on special assignments by their employers—for example, the airline involved, the manufacturer of the downed plane, and the pilots' and flight engineers' unions—to work with the detectives of the sky.

Obviously, each of these specialists may have a vested interest in the outcome of the investigation. A manufacturing company, while anxious to avoid blame for poor workmanship, nonetheless wants to help find any failings in its airliners, to prevent future tragedies. The NTSB procedure makes use of the expertise of the manufacturer, airline, crew members' unions, and others while seeking to ensure that nobody will be unjustifiably accused of causing an accident.

The ten subject areas into which the investigative teams are divided are given below, along with some of the key questions they try to answer.

Structures. Was the plane intact when it crashed? Was there a fire? If the crash resulted from a structural failure in the plane, what was it that failed?

Systems. Was the electrical system in the plane working properly at the time of the crash? What about the hydraulic system? Did the crew have full use of the controls?

Power Plants. Did one or more engines fail? If so, why?

Recorders. Airliners carry flight recorders—devices that automatically compile data concerning the planes' performance in flight—and tape recorders that monitor cockpit conversations. These recorders are built so sturdily that they can withstand the destructive forces of plane crashes. The first items investigators try to find in crash wreckage, after making sure that any survivors have been rescued, are the recorders. Often the devices provide valuable clues to the causes of air accidents.

Maintenance Records. Did the plane involved have a history of mechanical troubles? The investigators check the aircraft's maintenance records to see what sort of problems it has had and whether adequate repairs have been made. They also check the operating records of similar aircraft to determine whether certain mechanical problems arise with abnormal frequency on those planes.

After engine wreckage has been assembled from an accident site, the "power plants" group of an investigating team examines it for clues. These engines are from a Delta DC-8 that crashed on March 30, 1967, on approach to New Orleans.

Operations. Did the crash result from poor flying skill by the crew? Or did the crew almost succeed in making an emergency landing of a hopelessly crippled plane? Are changes needed in flight procedures?

Air-Traffic Control. Was the airliner flying at the proper altitude and on the proper course immediately before the crash? Was it given the right instructions by controllers on the ground? Was the ground radar system, used to keep track of planes' flight paths, operating properly at the time

of the crash? Such questions are especially important when
two or more planes collide in the air, but they must also be
answered in single-plane crashes.

Witnesses. All those known to have witnessed the accident, including crew members and passengers who may
survive the crash, are interviewed. What they saw or heard
may provide valuable theories on the cause of the accident.
Often, because of the shock of the event, such witnesses'
memories are faulty. With their permission, some of them
occasionally are questioned under hypnosis or drugs that
help bring to the surface details they would not otherwise
be able to remember. Investigators say such techniques
have helped unravel the mysteries surrounding the causes
of several crashes.

Weather. Were there any weather conditions—such as
thunderstorms, snow, or fog—that could have contributed
to the accident? How accurate were the weather forecasts
on which the plane's flight plan was based? Was the crew
kept informed by radio of changes in weather conditions?

Human Factors. This category runs a broad gamut. Could
the pilot have suffered a heart attack or other fatal seizure?
Did any passenger carry an unusually large amount of
flight insurance? Were there any other clues indicating possible sabotage? Autopsies on the bodies of crash victims
sometimes provide vital information. For example, evidence that the victims had inhaled substantial amounts of
smoke before their deaths might indicate the plane had caught
fire in the air.

Although these ten areas of investigation are pursued
after all major crashes, other procedures followed by the
detectives of the sky vary—depending on the circumstances
of each accident. In some cases, investigators reenact the
fatal flight with an identical plane following the ill-fated

aircraft's assigned course. In other cases, where weather conditions are suspected of contributing to the crash, those conditions are simulated in wind-tunnel tests designed to measure stresses on the aircraft.

Often, tiny clues can lead to solution of the mysteries of what causes planes to crash. Smoke patterns on a rivet head can indicate, for instance, that a plane caught fire in the air. Laboratory examination of the plane's interior can pinpoint where the fire started, and analysis of soot deposits can suggest what sort of materials burned.

Engines recovered from the crash wreckage are moved to a shop—often at the manufacturer's factory—where equipment is available to take them apart and give them minute examinations to determine whether they played any role in causing the accident. The kind of damage done to an engine will sometimes provide a vital clue. In the case of a propeller engine, the propeller blades bend forward if the engine is running when it strikes the ground. But if the engine is not running at the time, the blades peel back in the manner of a banana skin. In the case of a jet engine, bent rotor blades inside the motor can indicate that a malfunction occurred in flight.

On occasion, examination of one small piece of metal can provide the tip-off to the cause of the crash. In one case in which a jetliner crashed in Maryland, a tiny section of a wing tip gave such a clue. Investigators found minuscule pit marks on the wing tips. Laboratory tests revealed that the scars had been made when lightning struck the plane. Although lightning is often suspected of contributing to crashes, further investigation usually finds some other cause. In this case, however, the investigation determined that the lightning had ignited a mixture of fuel and air in a reserve fuel tank—touching off an explosion that had destroyed the wing and caused the plane to crash. Later models of the plane were redesigned to reduce the hazard of another lightning-induced crash. As will be seen, such remedial action following numerous tragedies has helped save countless lives.

Although they do not normally carry guns—except for protection against animals in rugged terrain—and do not make arrests, the NTSB investigators face many physical hazards in their work. They often must resort to dangerous means to reach crash sites and conduct their investigations. Even when the work is not hazardous, it is often exhausting. It requires individuals who can maintain their composure even in the face of gruesome sights—mangled bodies, crushed wreckage, and the like.

One case that posed unusual problems for the NTSB investigators involved the mystery surrounding a crash in the murky swamps of the Florida Everglades. To reach the wreckage, they rented a flat-bottomed marsh boat and poled their way to the crash site. When one of them stepped out of the boat onto the wing of the downed plane, he noticed a slight movement near his feet. He froze. Coiled a few feet from his boots were two venomous water moccasins—poised to strike. The investigator gingerly reached for one of the poles used to propel the boat. Then, with one swift sweep of the pole, he knocked both snakes into the water. They swam away. But the investigators had no way of knowing how many other water moccasins or other dangerous creatures might be inside the half-submerged cabin of the plane. Nonetheless, they had no choice except to crawl inside the cabin and give it an inch-by-inch inspection. It was the only way to carry out their assigned work.

Another crash occurred in a seemingly inaccessible region in the Rocky Mountains. To reach the scene, the investigators formed mountain burro pack teams and climbed the peaks wearing snowshoes and carrying rifles and heavy camping equipment. They found the wrecked plane buried in snow almost 12,000 feet above sea level.

Still another mountain crash posed even more difficult problems. The crash site could not be reached on foot. The investigators used a helicopter in an attempt to land on a peak near the wreckage. This was a hazardous measure, since such a helicopter had never flown so high carrying such a heavy cargo of equipment. But, again, there seemed no choice. The helicopter managed to land safely on the peak. The investigators then lowered ropes down the face of a sheer cliff and slid down with their equipment to begin the investigation. When finished with their work at the wreckage site, they had to climb back up the ropes along the side of the cliff to reach the point where they could be picked up by the helicopter.

When another airliner plunged to the bottom of a lake on an estate near Jacksonville, Florida, three detectives of the sky took a cram course in skin diving in preparation for the investigation. They then dived to the lake bottom with acetylene torches, cut their way into the wreckage, and examined it in the same painstaking detail they would have if the plane had crashed on land.

Some of the NTSB investigators' most difficult assignments have involved crashes in the rugged terrain of foreign countries. In one such case, an American-owned airliner crashed deep in the jungles of Honduras. The investigators —after assembling such equipment as jungle boots, snake-proof pants, machetes, axes, mosquito netting, and drugs to combat tropical diseases—had to hack their way through the jungle for five days to reach the crash site. They then had to clear a temporary road for jeeps loaded with investigative equipment. Despite the problems of conducting an investigation under such conditions, they got the job done.

Of course, finding the cause of a crash is only one of many factors entering into the overall issue of aviation safety. Nothing is more frustrating to the NTSB investigators than to pinpoint a dangerous situation and make recommendations for eliminating it—only to see their recommendations ignored and another plane crash result. Chapter 3 will explore just such a case and its tragic consequences, but it will be helpful to understand first the role played by the NTSB investigators within the larger complex of federal agencies responsible for regulating the aviation industry.

A wing breaks off an airliner, sending the plane into a dive that ends with everyone aboard killed. A short time later, it happens again on an identical aircraft. The flying public panics and becomes reluctant to fly on such planes. The mystery of what causes the wings to break off remains unsolved for an extended period. But finally the detectives of the sky, working with the plane's manufacturer and other aviation experts, solve the riddle. Corrections are made, and the airliner in question becomes one of the safest in the skies. (This remarkable case will be discussed in chapter 4.)

The records of such achievements fill one filing cabinet after another in the National Transportation Safety Board's headquarters in the sleek new Department of Transportation building on Washington's Independence Avenue, midway between the Capitol and the White House. But the NTSB did not always have the comfortable, well-equipped facilities it has now. In fact, the NTSB is a relatively new government agency. And its predecessor agency, the Civil Aeronautics Board Bureau of Safety, was not organized until a little more than three decades ago.

Over the years, vast changes have taken place in the aviation industry. Airlines have, for the most part, replaced their old propeller-driven planes with jetliners. Many more planes are in the sky than when the Civil Aeronautics Board (CAB) was formed in 1940. They are much larger and fly much faster than their predecessors. Thus the problems of keeping air travel safe have grown increasingly complex. To keep pace with the problems, changes have been made within the government agencies assigned to oversee air safety.

These adjustments mirror the short history of air travel. Many individuals, particularly young people, take air transportation—even space-vehicle travel to the moon—for granted. But it was not until the period following World War I, fewer than sixty years ago, that commercial aviation began to blossom as an industry. The initial growth of the industry was rapid and haphazard. Airlines sprung into being and were allowed to operate in chaotic fashion. Numerous crashes and disputes over such issues as plane fares, cargo rates, and government airmail subsidies kept the industry in seemingly constant turmoil. Finally, after U.S. senator Bronson Cutting of New Mexico was killed in an airline crash, Congress decided in 1938 that the time had come for the federal government to exercise broad control over commercial aviation.

The result was passage of a new law, called the Civil Aeronautics Act, which created an agency known as the Civil Aeronautics Administration to supervise and regulate the aviation industry. Within two years it became apparent that the CAA, as initially organized, was too cumbersome to operate efficiently. As a result, it was split into two separate agencies. One of them, renamed the Civil Aeronautics Authority, was part of the executive branch, reporting to the White House. The duties of the new CAA included developing and operating the nation's air-traffic control system (for example, providing the personnel and equipment used in airport control towers), developing civil air regulations, and licensing aviators and aircraft. The second agency, known as the Civil Aeronautics Board (CAB), reported to Congress. Its functions included establishing airline routes, setting passenger fares and freight rates, and determining the causes of aircraft accidents and making recommendations on safety improvements.

The CAB Bureau of Safety was created to carry out the crash investigations and other studies aimed at preventing aircraft accidents. The bureau's early investigators, the first detectives of the sky, had no precedents to guide them in their work. They were forced to invent their own investigative methods as they went along. Nonetheless, within only a few years, they managed to develop sophisticated techniques for uncovering the causes of crashes. They pioneered, for example, in using X-ray equipment to examine airplane parts for signs of metal fatigue, a condition in which the metal is weakened and likely to break under stress; in making use of medical, metallurgical, and other research laboratories to find clues to causes of crashes; and in devising systematic means of reconstructing the events leading up to an accident.

In 1958, to keep pace with the increasing size and complexity of the aviation industry, Congress passed a new law called the Federal Aviation Act. The law left intact the CAB Bureau of Safety's jurisdiction over crash investigations. But it established a new governmental unit, the Federal Aviation Agency (FAA), to replace the Civil Aeronautics Administration and exercise broader supervision over the aviation industry. The law directed the CAB to make recommendations to the FAA on how to prevent accidents. But it did not require the FAA to follow those recommendations. The FAA would ultimately be accused of laxity in failing to pursue safety suggestions from the CAB, thus increasing the risk of additional crashes.

A further reshuffling of the government agencies over-
seeing the aviation industry took place in 1966 when a
new cabinet-level Department of Transportation was established. The Federal Aviation Agency was renamed the Federal Aviation Administration and placed under the jurisdiction of the secretary of transportation. The CAB Bureau
of Safety was abolished. In its place, a new agency named
the National Transportation Safety Board (NTSB) was
created. Most of the detectives of the sky who had formerly
worked for the Bureau of Safety simply were transferred to
the NTSB. In addition to performing the duties formerly
carried out by the Bureau of Safety, the NTSB was also empowered to investigate certain other transportation accidents
such as train and bus crashes. But its major responsibility has
remained in aviation safety. Although some administrative
functions of the new transportation safety board are per-
formed by the Department of Transportation, the NTSB is
an independent agency reporting directly to Congress.

The CAB has remained in existence since the 1966 reor-
ganization, but has concentrated on economic matters af-
fecting the aviation industry and has played no further part
in supervising air safety. Under the new system, the NTSB
detectives of the sky investigate every important civilian
plane crash. When they have completed their work, their
evidence is presented at public hearings presided over by
an NTSB official known as a hearing examiner. Also taking part in the hearings are representatives of various other
organizations with interests in the case—including the airline involved, the plane's manufacturer, and airline-em-
ployee unions such as the Air Line Pilots Association and
the Flight Engineers International Association. After the
hearings, the examiner submits a report on the probable
cause of the crash to the five appointed members of the
NTSB. The board, which can accept or reject the examiner's

findings, then issues a final report determining the accident's probable cause. Such reports often contain recommendations to the FAA and other organizations on safety-improvement measures. But the NTSB, like the old CAB Bureau of Safety, has no power to compel compliance with these recommendations. Thus further reform seems necessary.

The deadliest aviation catastrophe in history occurred on March 3, 1974. A wide-bodied DC-10 jetliner owned by Turkish Airlines took off from Orly Airport outside Paris bound for London's Heathrow Airport, only an hour's flight away. But eleven minutes after takeoff, the plane crashed into a game refuge —killing 345 persons, including 22 Americans. The tragic irony was that the crash could have been averted if previous recommendations by the detectives of the sky had been followed.

Within two hours after the crash, Edward (Doug) Dreifus, a National Transportation Safety Board crash expert, was at a Washington airport with two colleagues boarding a flight to the crash scene. Although French authorities had primary responsibility for investigating the accident because it had taken place in their country, the NTSB detectives of the sky had partial jurisdiction since the airliner had been built by McDonnell Douglas Aircraft Corporation in Long Beach, California.

Doug Dreifus had viewed the remains of many wrecked planes during his three decades in the aviation field. He had been a Marine Corps pilot for twenty-one years, an airline safety officer for five years, and an NTSB investigator for four years. He had inspected in detail the wreckage of more than fifty large airliners. But the destruction he found at the French crash site was the worst he had ever seen.

A Turkish Airlines DC-10 slashed a path through heavily wooded terrain when it crashed in France on March 3, 1974. Investigators could tell from the crash site that the plane was under some sort of control when it hit the ground.

Pieces of the main sections of the airliner were scattered by the thousands over a half-mile area. The largest chunk still in one piece was only about ten by seventeen feet. In most plane crashes the tail remains reasonably intact. But in this case the tail had been smashed to bits.

Dreifus began his investigation by touring the entire area surrounding the crash scene on foot. "I went the whole distance the first visit, but piecemeal," he recalls. "Walk a bit, then think about what I'd seen. Then go back and look again to be sure. Then I'd walk some more and come back. I started about two-thirty in the afternoon and it was getting dark when I left, about six-thirty, that first day. Takes a while—rugged terrain. Getting ideas all the way. You get many thoughts, of course, as you see portions of the wreckage. But that doesn't obstruct your primary course of looking for everything."

It was immediately apparent to Dreifus that the plane had struck the ground at very high speed. It had sheared off huge trees on its way as if they had been sliced by a high-powered buzz saw. "I also knew the pilot wasn't in a spiral or a spin because of the nature of the wreckage. I knew immediately that the aircraft was under some sort of control."

The condition of the victims' bodies—battered into many pieces—also attested to the extreme force with which the plane had struck the ground. "Normally, on a major accident, by the time we get there the bodies have been removed," Dreifus says. "It's very unusual on a large major accident for the bodies to still be there. But this plane hit at a very high G-force [gravity force], high speed. They [the bodies] were really torn up [and thus took an abnormal length of time to remove]. But things like that you condition yourself to. It doesn't especially bother me. It's something you fear will get to you at first, and then you develop—well, you look at the bodies technically."

Examination of victims' bodies—while unpleasant—can provide important clues to the circumstances of a crash. "Take a typical spin accident," Dreifus explains. "If you're not sure the tail is in a spin, you might be able to tell by the fact that a victim has a twisted broken back. Or, for instance, if you're not sure who was flying the aircraft, a good pathologist [a doctor who specializes in diagnosis

A French official with the flight recorder just after it was recovered from the wreckage of the Turkish Airlines jetliner.

and often conducts autopsies] could tell by the nature of injuries to the hands—say, they are broken in a certain manner—if they were on the controls at the time of the accident."

Dreifus and other investigators found a major clue to the cause of the Turkish airliner's crash when they discovered the plane's rear cargo door, plus the bodies of six victims, nine miles south-southeast of the main wreckage. That discovery alerted them to striking parallels between the crash in France and an earlier accident investigated by the NTSB. As Edward Slattery, veteran public-information director for the NTSB, puts it: "Right away, we saw the total similarity of the accident in France with a case we had handled in Windsor, Ontario, Canada. You had the door several miles behind the scene of impact, so you knew it came off in flight. And you had six people lying around in what we call freefall; they fell free, so their bodies weren't mangled. It was the rear cargo door—we were pinpointing it like beagle dogs."

The earlier accident with characteristics similar to the crash in France had taken place on June 12, 1972. American Airlines Flight 96—a DC-10 virtually identical to the Turkish Airlines jetliner—was en route from Los Angeles to New York with intermediate stops in Detroit and Buffalo. After the stop in Detroit, the plane was climbing at an altitude of 11,750 feet on its way to Buffalo when its rear bulk-cargo compartment door blew off without warning over Windsor, Ontario.

Pilot Bryce McCormick, copilot Peter Whitney, and flight engineer Clayton Burke heard and felt a thud at that point. Simultaneously, dust and dirt flew up into their faces, the rudder pedals moved to the full left-rudder position, and the plane curved to the right. Pilot McCormick momentarily lost his vision. He did not realize the cargo door had blown off, and thought the plane had suffered a midair collision.

After regaining his vision, McCormick disengaged the automatic-pilot device—which had been operating the plane at the time the door blew off—and took manual control of the airliner. He found that two of the three engines responded when he applied power. But the third engine, mounted in the tail, did not respond because a lever had been jammed. McCormick discovered that many of the plane's controls would perform only sluggishly and that the rudder control would not work at all. The airliner continued curving to the right. McCormick declared an emergency, asking air-traffic controllers to clear him for a return to Detroit's Metropolitan—Wayne County Airport and an emergency landing.

Meanwhile, in the passenger cabin, most of the plane's seven flight attendants and fifty-six passengers heard a loud noise when the door blew off, then saw what appeared to be fog in the cabin. The pressurized air within the cabin rushed out through the open doorway, and the floor of the plane's rear lounge area collapsed, falling partially into the cargo compartment. Two flight attendants seated near the rear of the plane were thrown to the floor and received minor injuries, but were able to join their five colleagues in attending to the passengers. Their main concern was to be sure that the passengers were properly using the oxygen masks that had automatically deployed in front of their seats when the cabin suddenly lost air pressure. (Such masks are necessary for normal breathing when a plane suffers a loss of pressurization at a high altitude.) The flight attendants, on instructions from the cockpit, also gave the passengers instructions on crash-landing and emergency evacuation procedures.

Despite the airliner's crippled condition, the crew was able to control it sufficiently well to proceed to an emergency landing pattern approaching the Detroit airport. At McCormick's request, the control tower cleared him for an abnormally long and gradual descent. Through skillful use of his two remaining engines and those controls that were still functioning, McCormick managed to maneuver the plane down to a runway. But both he and copilot Whitney had to apply full back pressure to the controls to get the airliner to slow down as it landed.

Immediately upon touching the ground, the plane veered sharply to the right off the runway. McCormick slammed his engines into reverse, but the jetliner continued swerving to the right. Whitney, on McCormick's instructions, took the right engine out of reverse and applied even greater reverse pressure on the left engine. That maneuver helped control the plane's direction, and it ran along the ground parallel to the runway for about 2,800 feet before it began a gradual left turn back to the runway. It finally came to rest 8,800 feet from the beginning of the runway. The nose and left main landing gear were on the runway surface, and the right main landing gear was off the runway surface.

As soon as the airliner came to rest, McCormick ordered an emergency evacuation. The plane's evacuation slides were deployed, and crew members helped the passengers slide down to the ground. Nine passengers suffered minor injuries, either during the turbulence of the in-flight loss of air pressure or during the evacuation.

But a major catastrophe had been averted, chiefly because of the skill of the crew. The NTSB, after investigating the accident, praised members of the cockpit crew "for the manner in which they successfully coped with the unusual in-flight emergency." The board also commended the flight attendants "for their actions, which are indicative of excellent training and a high professional attitude."

In seeking the cause of the accident, NTSB investigators quickly determined that the rapid air depressurization caused by the loss of the cargo compartment door had collapsed the floor of the rear passenger lounge. When the floor had fallen, it had severed or damaged most of the flight-control cables leading to the plane's tail section. But the main question was what had caused the cargo door to blow off in the first place.

The investigators discovered that, after cargo had been loaded aboard the plane in Detroit, a ground crewman had experienced trouble in closing the door. On the large door itself was a smaller vent door. When the ground crewman tried to shut the vent door, he could not get its handle to move into the closed position by using normal force. He applied additional force with his knee. This seemed to push the handle into the proper position, but the crewman noticed that the vent door was closed in a slightly cocked manner. The crewman brought the matter to the attention of a mechanic, who nonetheless cleared the plane for takeoff.

Among the devices on flight engineer Burke's instrument board was a panel designed to light up if any cargo door was not properly secured for flight. But Burke told the investigators that this light had never come on either during flight preparations or the flight itself.

The detectives of the sky conducted extensive tests on the cargo doors of other DC-10s. They discovered the design of the door-latching mechanism was such that the door could appear to be locked when it actually was not. They also found that, under certain conditions, the warning light on the flight engineer's instrument panel would fail to come on even though the door was not locked. The investigators concluded, as they put it in their report on the accident, that "the crew had no warning that the door mechanism was not functioning properly."

As the plane climbed into the sky, the difference in air pressure between the pressurized cargo compartment and the air outside caused the failure of fasteners holding the cargo door in place. The door latches sprung open, permitting the door to blow off. The official report on the cause of the accident said:

The National Transportation Safety Board determines that the probable cause of this accident was the improper engagement of the latching mechanism for the aft bulk cargo compartment door during the preparation of the

*airplane for flight. The design characteristics of the door
latching mechanism permitted the door to be apparently
closed when, in fact, the latches were not fully engaged
and the latch lockpins were not in place.*

In an attempt to prevent similar accidents from occurring
in the future, the NTSB recommended to the Federal Aviation Administration on July 6, 1972, that several safety
modifications be required on all DC-10s. One recommendation called for requiring adjustment of the DC-10 locking
mechanism "to make it physically impossible to position
the external locking handle and vent door to their normal
door-locked positions unless the locking pins are fully engaged." Another urged installation of additional vents
above the cargo compartment to minimize the result of any
sudden loss of air pressure.

As previously explained, the NTSB is empowered only
to make recommendations. It is up to the FAA to follow up
on those recommendations. In this case, the FAA declined
to abide by the NTSB suggestions. Only a day after receiving them, FAA administrator J. H. Shaffer informed the
NTSB of an alternate procedure under which companies
using DC-10s were being permitted to conduct their own
tests of the door mechanisms and to make any changes they
deemed necessary. Shaffer wrote NTSB chairman John H.
Reed: "While a preliminary investigation indicates that it
may not be feasible to provide complete venting between
cabin and cargo compartments, your recommendations will
be considered. . . ."

In other words, the FAA was permitting the aviation
industry to regulate itself—instead of insisting on safety improvements recommended by the NTSB experts. Airlines
and aircraft manufacturers, while they obviously have a
vested interest in safety, often are reluctant to make me-

chanical changes in their equipment unless required to do so. Such changes can be costly, and the aviation industry is naturally determined to keep its expenses to a minimum.

What resulted was that the DC-10 manufacturer, the McDonnell Douglas Aircraft Corporation, issued an informal notice called a service bulletin to companies using the plane. The service bulletin suggested certain modifications on the plane, but did not adopt all of the NTSB recommendations. Moreover, the manufacturer's suggestions were optional. Had the FAA issued an order requiring implementation of the NTSB recommendations, that order would have had the force of law.

Even the lesser modifications suggested by McDonnell Douglas were for some reason not made on the DC-10 that eventually crashed in France, even though the plane had not yet been delivered to Turkish Airlines at the time the manufacturer recommended the design changes. Nonetheless, the FAA issued the plane a document known as an "airworthiness certificate," which indicated that the aircraft was safe and could be used in airline service.

Later investigation of the crash in France determined that the accident had begun as a virtual replay of the mishap over Windsor, Ontario. The cargo compartment door had blown off and the passenger cabin floor had collapsed in the same manner as those on the American Airlines plane. Since all crew members of the Turkish Airlines plane had been killed, it was impossible to determine precisely what had happened next. But two possibilities seemed most logical. Either the Turkish Airlines jumbo jet had suffered an even greater loss of its controls than the American Airlines plane or the Turkish Airlines crew had shown less skill in flying the crippled aircraft than had the American Airlines crew.

In any event, 345 persons had lost their lives. And their

deaths apparently could have been prevented. As one
NTSB official put it, "That accident wouldn't have happened if our recommendations had been followed."

Following the investigation of the crash in France, the
FAA was subjected to sharp criticism from various quarters
for its failure to take stronger action in the DC-10 affair and
other cases involving potential safety hazards. A congressional subcommittee, for example, conducted an extensive
study of air-safety measures and accused the FAA of "slug-
gishness which at times approaches an attitude of indif-
ference to public safety." The House [of Representatives]
Special Subcommittee on Investigations, headed by Con-
gressman Harley C. Staggers of West Virginia, said the FAA
had "needlessly and unjustifiably put at risk" thousands of
lives by failing to deal properly with the NTSB recommendations for improvements on the DC-10. "Administrative
delay and inactivity is bad in any agency," the subcommittee said in its report "In the case of the FAA, it may literally
endanger human life. Instances of completely inappropriate
bureaucratic slowness to act, and inaction, are noted throughout this report."

Another critique, prepared by the U.S. General Accounting Office (GAO), accused the FAA of ignoring
many NTSB recommendations, delaying action on others,
and losing the files on some. The GAO, a congressional
watchdog agency, said the secretary of transportation
should establish tighter controls to assure that the FAA
acted promptly on NTSB recommendations and followed
up to see that its actions produced safety improvements.
From 1970 through 1974, the GAO report said, the
NTSB made 655 aviation-safety recommendations to the
FAA. It said that 222 of those had never been acted upon
and were still classified as "open." Because of inadequate

FAA procedures, the report said, "recommendations have not been resolved promptly and have been forgotten."

The FAA appointed an inquiry board of its own to conduct an internal investigation aimed at assessing the agency's performance in the DC-10 affair. Heading the ten-member board was Oscar Bakke, a former detective of the sky who had become FAA associate administrator for aviation safety. The board found that the FAA had been "ineffective" in dealing with the NTSB safety recommendations and had taken "questionable" actions in certifying the Turkish Airlines plane as safe.

Not until July 1975, three years after the NTSB had initially recommended the modifications on the DC-10s, did the FAA finally get around to ordering mandatory safety improvements. The FAA directed manufacturers and operators of DC-10s and two other jumbo jets, the Boeing 747 and Lockheed L-1011, to make design changes enabling the planes to withstand sudden fuselage openings of at least twenty square feet and still land safely.

The design changes involve expansion of the vent systems and strengthening of doors. It will cost an estimated $200,000 to make the improvements on each of the 275 jumbo jets currently operated by this country's airlines, but the expense will be considerably less on new planes yet to come off the assembly lines.

NTSB officials, however, considered the modifications ordered by the FAA inadequate. While the FAA order made it necessary for the planes to withstand fuselage openings of only twenty square feet, the NTSB noted, some doors on jumbo jets are as large as sixty-one square feet. If one of these large doors unexpectedly opened in flight, the NTSB contended, the new FAA regulations might be insufficient to protect the aircraft. The NTSB urged more thorough safety analysis to "demonstrate that [protection against] hull openings greater than twenty feet need not be considered." It also recommended action to provide better protection for the jumbo jets' control systems or installation of emergency control systems. At this writing, the conflict between the views of the FAA and the NTSB remains unresolved.

Obviously, the accomplishments of the detectives of the sky in solving the mysteries of plane crashes are worthless when soundly based recommendations for preventing future disasters are ignored or subverted. Measures are currently being taken—as a result of congressional investigation, government overhaul, and industry soul-searching—to try to ensure that NTSB recommendations are pursued more diligently in the future. The lives of hundreds—perhaps thousands—of airline passengers and crew members may well depend on the success or failure of these reforms.

If ever a certain airliner model seemed to be jinxed, that model was the Electra turboprop plane developed by Lockheed Aircraft Corporation. Within a two-year period ending in the early 1960s, no fewer than six Electras were involved in disastrous accidents. The crashes touched off a mild panic among airline passengers, many of whom refused to fly aboard Electras. Solving the mystery of what was causing the Electras to crash presented the detectives of the sky with one of their most difficult cases.

Extensive investigation of the accidents revealed that, in four of them, the fact that the planes involved were Electras was merely coincidental. Those crashes were not caused by any basic failing in the aircraft; they could have happened to any airliner. But such was not the case with the two other accidents. Those two bore striking similarities, and the indications were that some inadequacy in the Electras' performance had been responsible for the tragedies. Pinpointing the precise nature of the inadequacy, however, proved to be exceedingly troublesome.

The Electra was the first turboprop plane capable of flying at speeds of more than 400 miles an hour. As a result, pilots faced new problems in flying it. For example, a pilot unexpectedly encountering air turbulence in a slower plane would usually be able to slow his plane to minimize the effect on his aircraft, passengers, and crew. But, in an Electra, he would have the same chance of slow-ing his plane suddenly as a motorist would have of stopping his car on a dime while driving at 75 miles an hour.

The first of the two puzzling crashes occurred on September 29, 1959. Braniff Airways Flight 542, an Electra carrying twenty-eight passengers and six crew membrs, took off from the airport in Houston, Texas, at 10:44 P.M. for its nightly flight to Dallas. The takeoff was thirty-two minutes behind schedule because of minor repairs made to the electrical system of one of the plane's engines.

In command of the airliner was Braniff captain Wilson Stone, a veteran pilot. He and his copilot, Dan Hollowell, checked in periodically during the flight with air-traffic controllers in Houston, San Antonio, and Fort Worth. They reported all was proceeding normally. At 11:05 P.M., the plane radioed that it was passing over Leona, Texas.

Five minutes later, a motorist driving a convertible near Buffalo, Texas, saw a light flash through the sky. There was an orange glow that seemed to grow in size and brightness, then fade. This was followed by a deafening blast that sounded like an explosion. Nearby, state highway patrolman J. B. Kyle was asleep in his home. "I was in bed and was awakened by a noise which sounded like a jet plane flying low over the house," Kyle would eventually tell the detectives of the sky. Kyle said he then heard a noise that sounded something like thunder. "I raised up and looked out the window and saw a large red glare in the sky," he recalled. "I figured a jet plane from some Air Force base had crashed, so I went to my [patrol] car and radioed Waco to check with the Air Force to see if they had a plane in the area. In just a matter of minutes, Mr. White [a neighbor, Richard White] called me and advised that part of that plane was in his backyard. I went to his place and, as soon as we got to the crash scene, I could see enough lettering on a section of the plane to recognize that it was a Braniff plane."

Both wreckage and the bodies of victims were found in a potato patch on White's property, and on nearby land. Fragments of the airliner were strewn over an area nearly three miles long. It was apparent that the plane's wings had come off in flight and that the remainder of the aircraft had plunged to the ground with a terrific impact. All thirty-four persons aboard had been killed.

The investigators assigned to find the cause of the crash established that the left wing of the Electra had broken off first. The break had come at the root of the wing, near the plane's fuselage. But the investigators could find no obvious reason why such a break should have occurred. All the radio reports from the crew had indicated the flight was proceeding toward Dallas in routine fashion. As far as was known, the weather had been clear in the area of the accident. Moreover, the Electra was a plane that had been tested against structural failure as rigorously as any aircraft in history. It met or exceeded all FAA requirements for structural performance and strength. Yet it was obvious some structural problem had caused the breaking of the wing.

In an attempt to locate that problem, all kinds of new tests were conducted on Electras. The planes were subjected to experiments in which stresses far greater than those likely to be encountered in airline flight were exerted on the wings and other sections. In all cases, the planes remained intact. The investigators were baffled, but continued with their tests.

On March 17, 1960, while the Texas accident was still under investigation, another Electra crashed in a similar fashion. This plane, Northwest Orient Airlines Flight 710,

had flown from Minneapolis to Chicago and then taken off
for Miami. There were six crew members and fifty-seven
passengers aboard. Among the passengers were several
well-known persons—including Chicago superior court
judge John A. Sbarbaro; millionaire businessman R. L.
Oare; Mrs. Morris Chalfen, wife of the producer of the
Hollywood on Ice revues; and Leland Watson, president of
a large electronics firm.

Commanding the flight was Northwest captain Ed La-
Parle. At 3 P.M., LaParle radioed air-traffic controllers at
Indianapolis that he was flying at 18,000 feet and everything seemed normal. Twenty minutes later, a farmer
named Albert J. Harpe who lived near Tell City, Indiana,
was standing in his yard when he heard a noise that
"sounded as if shotgun shells were exploding, only some-
what louder." He looked up and saw Flight 710, then
thought he heard the plane's motors stop. Next he saw one
of the plane's wings—which was on fire—falling to the
ground.

Another farmer who lived nearby, Theodore Wilson,
was standing on his porch when he heard what sounded
like an explosion. He ran to the porch railing, looked up,
and saw the main section of the airliner falling toward the
ground. It rammed into the earth a few hundred feet beyond his property line.

The wrecked Electra had plunged toward the ground at
a speed close to 600 miles an hour. When it had struck, the
impact had been so great that the plane's fuselage—more
than one hundred feet long—had been buried beneath the
soggy earth of a soybean field. The plane had dug a crater
ten feet deep and twenty-five feet wide through the field.
Rescue workers were obliged to dig through the earth to un-
cover the wreckage and the bodies of the sixty-three victims.

A state policeman (right) watches as a NTSB investigator examines a piece of wreckage from the crater made when a Northwest Airlines Electra crashed near Tell City, Indiana, in 1960. It took nine months of investigations to discover the cause of the accident.

Following as it did the crash near Buffalo, Texas, the Tell City accident spurred even more intensive efforts by investigators to solve the riddle of the Electra's fatal flaw.

More than ever, in view of the fact that a wing had broken off the plane that had crashed near Tell City, the detectives of the sky were convinced there was a structural defect in the Electra. But they remained temporarily stymied in efforts to find that defect.

At hearings into the cause of the Tell City crash, the investigators heard testimony that the Northwest Electra had made an unusually bumpy landing in Chicago just before taking off on the ill-fated flight for Miami. One of the witnesses who provided such testimony was Sidney J. Kaplan, an attorney who had ridden on the plane from Minneapolis to Chicago. An investigator at the hearing asked him, "Do you recall anything unusual or out of the ordinary about the flight from the time it left Minneapolis until you arrived in Chicago?"

"I considered the flight uneventful, except the landing at Chicago."

Q: "Would you care to comment on the landing?"

A: "Yes. That landing was extremely bumpy. Immediately when we landed I turned to the passenger sitting to the left of me and remarked to him that this was the bumpiest landing that I could remember in my experience, and he expressed concurrence in that."

Q: "Could we go into that landing just a little bit more? That word 'bumpy,' would you describe it as rather a hard jar or possibly as a matter of skipping?"

A: "In a matter as serious as this, I would not want to press my recollection for details that may be elusive. I do remember very clearly and definitely that it was bumpy, extremely bumpy, and the detailed analysis of that may be something that I couldn't probably recall in detail and be accurate about it."

Q: "You have been a passenger on landings at Chicago forty times over a period of years?"
A: "I am reasonably certain that I have."
Q: "And this was the roughest landing of all?"
A: "It certainly was."

Kaplan's testimony was bolstered by that of another witness at the hearing, Arthur G. Janssen, a marketing executive who had also been aboard Flight 710 from Minneapolis to Chicago. Janssen also said he was a frequent airline passenger. An investigator asked, "Would you care to comment on the approach and landing [of Flight 710]?"

"Well, I might say that I have been flying since 1940, and I have only been scared three times and this was one of the times," Janssen replied. "We came into Chicago. It was overcast. . . . I was sitting way far back. I had an excellent view right under the wing. As we came over the landing strip, usually they come in and you are smack right on it. We went on in and we used up what I consider a fair amount of runway before we touched down. The plane was jarring . . . and we came down in this position [indicating with his hand that the plane was wobbling from side to side]. The wing, I know, did not touch the ground. But when we did hit it was on one wheel very definitely. It was one of those booms, and I don't know how long we were in this same identical position before the plane touched down on the other wheel. It may have been 200 yards. . . . I was scared. I grabbed the edge of my seat, and we had no more runway left when we finally came to a stop. You could feel that the pilot was having one heck of a job getting this thing stopped. . . . It was what I would consider a violent, jolting landing."

"You described the touchdown as jolting rather than—"

"Violent. I used the word violent."

"Violent?"

"Yes, [with the plane tilted] on one wheel."

The investigators also heard testimony that a weather condition known as clear-air turbulence was present at the time of the Tell City crash. Airline pilots were accustomed to dealing with the problem of air turbulence associated with thunderstorms and other foul-weather conditions. Since thunderstorms could be seen on radar, the pilots could try to fly around them or slow down when passing through them. Clear-air turbulence, however, did not show up on radar screens and thus was a more difficult problem. As previously noted, it would have been particularly troublesome for the pilot of an Electra to slow down after encountering clear-air turbulence.

Two Air Force pilots who had been flying above the Tell City area at the time of the Electra accident told of running into extreme clear-air turbulence. Captain John Karibo, who had been piloting an RB-57 bomber, said his plane had bucked so violently that he had been thrown against the cockpit canopy. "There was a sort of chuckhole roughness at first," Karibo told the investigators. "And then bang." Colonel Dan Shea, who had been flying an Air Force T-33 jet trainer, said he had also encountered such turbulence. The force was so great that it threw him out of his seat, he said.

Although they could not know it at the time, the testimony about the rough landing in Chicago and the clear-air turbulence would eventually provide the investigators with partial clues needed to solve the mystery of what had caused the Electras to crash. But that solution would take time to accomplish. While the riddle remained unsolved, the Civil Aeronautics Board took the drastic step of urging the FAA to ground all Electras until the structural problem could be discovered. At the time, 113 Electras were being used by U.S. airlines and 20 by foreign airlines. Those used in this country alone carried more than 25,000 passengers a day. FAA administrator Elwood (Pete) Quesada, a former Air Force general, was reluctant to pull all those planes out of service. He reasoned that, if he did so, the airlines would revert to using older planes that might have their own safety problems because of age. "Suppose I took the public out of Electras and got some of them killed in [older-model] DC-7s," Quesada said. As a result, he decided to keep the Electras in the air—but to order them flown at drastically reduced speeds as a precaution.

With many passengers refusing to fly in Electras, there was enormous pressure on the CAB investigators, the FAA, the plane's manufacturer, and the aviation industry in general to ferret out the cause of the accidents. The investigation intensified, with all elements of the industry pooling their efforts in a cooperative venture that reached unprecedented size and scope.

Under the supervision of the detectives of the sky, engineers from Lockheed conducted around-the-clock experiments to test the ability of Electra wings to endure all kinds of stresses. An Electra just off the assembly line was packed with electronic instruments capable of measuring with great precision the forces that air turbulence could exert on the wings and engines. The plane was flown into a mountainous region of California known for its extremely high winds. Test pilots spent weeks checking the effects of the wind currents on the plane at various speeds, altitudes, and directions.

Northwest Orient Airlines loaned the investigators an Electra that had been flown approximately the same number of hours as the plane involved in the Tell City crash.

Investigators put the plane through tests in which the wings were mechanically shaken at high speeds over long periods to check, among other things, their resistance to metal fatigue.

Finally, after thousands of tests had been conducted over a nine-month period, the investigators discovered a flaw in the Electras—not in the wings themselves but in the mountings that held the engines in place on the wings. They found that the mountings could be weakened by unusual stresses, such as those caused by extremely bumpy landings or violent air turbulence. Recalling the testimony about the hard landing and the clear-air turbulence at the hearings into the Tell City disaster, the investigators wondered whether weakening of the engine mountings could have caused the crash and the one in Texas.

A new model of an Electra wing, including an engine mounting and the engine itself, was constructed and subjected to wind-tunnel tests. The wing model was put through maneuvers in all directions as increasingly powerful wind forces were applied. No matter how much force was exerted, the wing itself remained undamaged. But the investigators noted that, when a simulated high speed was reached in the wind tunnel, the engine mounts weakened and the engine started to wobble. The vibrations caused by this wobbling spread to the wing. Some experts said the effect was similar to the vibration of a tuning fork. Others likened it to the spreading of ripples caused by a stone thrown into a body of water.

In any event, as the investigators watched, the model wing began to flutter violently up and down. After about a half minute, the wing broke off at the point where it would have joined the fuselage if it had been part of an entire plane. The mystery of the Electras had been solved.

All the Electras in service throughout the world were

ferried back to Lockheed's California factory for repairs to strengthen the engine mountings. New planes coming off the assembly line were built with reinforced mountings. The work cost Lockheed more than $25 million. But, from that time on, the Electra compiled a safety record as desirable as that of any plane in the sky.

No potential hazard is more frightening to an aviator or passenger than the danger of an airborne explosion. Because today's airliners fly with pressurized cabins to help those aboard breathe normally at high altitudes, any break in the fuselage—such as that caused by an explosion—may be fatal. Air rushing from the pressurized cabin can suck passengers and crew members out of the plane. Moreover, the rush of air itself can cause a plane to begin breaking up and eventually fall apart.

Thus the fear of sabotage—particularly of the planting of a bomb aboard an aircraft—haunts the aviation industry and the detectives of the sky. Although telephoned bomb scares are hardly rare, actual bombings of planes come few and far between. Nonetheless, those that do occur usually have tragic consequences. Only occasionally are there survivors of such bombings.

The first bombing case to receive nationwide attention took place on November 1, 1955, and presented the detectives of the sky with one of their most celebrated investigations. They did not know they were dealing with a case of sabotage; that information came only through patient detective work. Actually, it began rather routinely.

Conrad Hopp, a beet farmer, had finished his chores and was sitting down to dinner with his family in his home near Longmont, Colorado, when he heard a terrifying boom outdoors. He jumped up from the table and ran to his front door. Outside, he was startled to see the early night sky brightly lighted by a ball of fire dropping from the heavens.

Nearby, the shattering noise and blinding light also shocked Bob Robbins, a florist from Loveland, Colorado, who had been driving south to Denver. He watched the ball of fire fall to earth, then heard another loud boom.

A little more than thirty miles away, air-traffic controllers in the control tower at Denver's Stapleton Airport noticed two white lights, one brighter than the other appearing suddenly in the northwest sky. For thirty to forty-five seconds, they watched as the lights seemed to fall at approximately the same speed. Then they saw a momentary flash of light, at or near the ground, that illuminated the base of clouds about 10,000 feet in the air.

Alarmed, the controllers immediately began trying to determine whether any airplane in the general area of Denver was in trouble. Radio calls were put out to all aircraft known to be flying in the vicinity. With one exception, the crews of all the planes radioed back that they had no problems. The exception was United Air Lines Flight 629, a DC-6B that had left the Denver airport a short time earlier for Portland, Oregon. Despite repeated efforts, the controllers were unable to establish radio contact with Flight 629. What, they wondered, could have happened to it?

The answer—or at least a partial answer—was not long in coming. Within minutes, a woman who lived on a farm eight miles from Longmont telephoned the local sheriff's office and reported in a trembling voice, "A plane crashed on our place. It's exploded and there's a fire. You'd better send help!"

Ambulances, fire engines, and squad cars raced to the scene, but could not help the occupants of Flight 629. All

The tail assembly was the largest section found in one piece after a United DC-6B crashed near Longmont, Colorado, on November 1, 1955. The tail section was found almost a mile from the rest of the scattered wreckage.

thirty-nine passengers and five crew members had been killed. Emergency workers put out the fire and began the grim work of removing the victims' bodies from thousands of pieces of twisted wreckage.

Among those who soon converged on the Longmont area were members of the Civil Aeronautics Board (CAB) Bureau of Safety. They began their work by examining the wreckage strewn over the Colorado countryside, along a route leading north-northwest and covering about six square miles. The tail assembly was about 4,600 feet from two deep craters that contained large portions of both wings, the plane's four engines, and the main landing gear. Six hundred feet south of the craters, the investigators found the forward section of the plane's fuselage. The rear (or, in aircraft terminology, aft) part of the fuselage had been torn into bits and pieces that had been scattered over a wide path extending about four miles south-southeast of the main wing wreckage.

The investigators methodically began putting together a detailed sketch of the location of each piece of wreckage. A surveyor laid out a straight line through the scene of the crash in the direction that the airliner had been flying. Every 1,000 feet along that line, another line 1,000 feet long was drawn across it at right angles. The bisecting lines thus formed a grid of squares. Each square was numbered. And every piece of wreckage found within a square was marked, and its location in relation to other pieces noted.

When that work had been completed, the wreckage was transported to a warehouse in Denver and laid out on a smaller grid corresponding to the one at the crash scene. The investigators then constructed a model of the plane's fuselage, known as a mock-up, with wood and chicken wire. Each piece of identifiable wreckage from the fuselage was hung in place on the mock-up in the position it had occupied on the airliner before the crash.

Construction of the mock-up provided significant clues to the cause of the crash. It was quickly noted that the pieces of wreckage became progressively smaller from all directions as they approached a point in what had been the plane's No. 4 baggage compartment. Many pieces from that section were missing entirely. The investigators concluded the rear fuselage had disintegrated in the air from extremely violent forces that had originated in a concentrated area

Airlines official W. C. Mentzer points to the spot in the mock-up of the baggage compartment of the United jetliner where investigators believed an explosion had occurred.

within the baggage compartment. But what had caused these violent forces? To the investigators' trained eyes, it seemed obvious there had been an explosion.

This conclusion was bolstered by other evidence. Interviews with witnesses to the crash, for example, produced general agreement that there had been a loud noise such as that from an explosion while the plane had still been in the air. The investigators also noted that the forward fuselage assembly had struck the ground with great force in an upright position, indicating it had dropped almost vertically after the plane had come apart in the air. Moreover, smudge marks and odors characteristic of an explosion had been discovered on pieces of wreckage known to have come from the vicinity of the No. 4 baggage compartment. The marks and odors had been particularly pronounced on passenger baggage, mail sacks, and other items stowed in the compartment.

While trying to determine what could have caused the explosion, one team of investigators began tracing the history of Flight 629. On the day of the crash, the flight originated—as it did every day of the week—at La Guardia Airport in New York. It then flew to Chicago before arriving in Denver, from where it was scheduled to go to Portland and then end its journey in Seattle, Washington. The plane landed in Denver at 6:11 P.M., eleven minutes behind schedule. In Denver the airliner was refueled and a new crew came aboard to complete the flight. The crew consisted of Captain Lee H. Hall, who had been a pilot with United for fifteen years and had logged more than 10,000 hours in the air; copilot Donald A. White, who had been with the airline for five years; flight engineer Samuel F. Arthur, with nine years' experience; and flight attendants Peggy L. Peddicord and Jacqueline L. Hinds.

Aside from the refueling, Flight 629 required no maintenance work during the stopover in Denver. The No. 4 baggage compartment—which had initially held cargo, luggage, and mail bound for Denver from New York and Chicago—was completely emptied during the layover. It was then reloaded with fresh baggage and mail originating in Denver.

Captain Hall and other crew members received a routine briefing before takeoff. They were told among other things, that the weather conditions should pose no problems. By 6:44 P.M., Flight 629 was standing on an airport runway, receiving clearance from the control tower to take off for Portland. Eight minutes later, the plane was in the air. At 6:56, as scheduled, the crew radioed that the airliner was passing over the Denver radio station. Flight 629 was under instructions to report next by radio when it climbed to an altitude of 18,000 feet en route to its assigned flight altitude of 21,000 feet. But that report never came. The last word ever heard from the plane was the 6:56 radio message.

It was at 7:03 P.M. that the air-traffic controllers in the Denver control tower spotted lights falling toward earth in the northwest sky. The CAB investigators assumed that the lights were pieces of flaming wreckage, set afire by the suspected in-flight explosion.

In seeking the cause of the explosion, the investigators tried to determine whether such a blast could have been touched off by some malfunction in the airplane. But all the available evidence seemed to lead away from that possibility. For one thing, there was nothing of an explosive nature in the structure of the plane near the No. 4 baggage compartment, where the blast was presumed to have occurred. For another, even more distant sections of the plane that contained explosive materials—such as the fuel tanks— would not have been capable of triggering such an intense explosion as the one that had blown apart Flight 629. Moreover, detailed examination of the wreckage produced no indication of a malfunction leading to the explosion.

Seeking further clues, the CAB investigators sent pieces of the plane's wreckage and contents to a government laboratory for chemical analysis. It revealed that the sootlike smudges on wreckage from the No. 4 baggage compartment contained residues that could be expected from the explosion of dynamite containing sodium nitrate. Further analysis disclosed that other residues contained manganese dioxide—a major component of the mixture contained in dry-cell batteries. Eleven pieces of material that could have originated from an Eveready "Hot Shot" battery were identified. Both dynamite and batteries are used, of course, in certain types of bombs. The obvious conclusion was that a time bomb had exploded inside the No. 4 baggage compartment.

But who had planted the bomb aboard the plane? And why?

Since sabotage of an airliner is a federal crime that falls under the jurisdiction of the Federal Bureau of Investigation, FBI agents were assigned to help the CAB investigators find the answers to those questions. The two government agencies had overlapping responsibilities in the case. The CAB Bureau of Safety was in charge of determining the precise cause of the crash; the FBI, assuming that a crime had been committed, was responsible for arresting the guilty person or persons.

Investigations were launched into the backgrounds of the passengers and crew members killed in the crash. Because the No. 4 baggage compartment had been filled with baggage loaded on the plane in Denver, particular interest centered on passengers who had boarded the plane there. Could any of them have been the target of a murder plot?

The investigators' suspicions were aroused when no sign could be found of the luggage belonging to one passenger, Mrs. Daisie King, who had boarded in Denver. They knew Mrs. King had taken a large suitcase with her to the airport. Airline records showed, in fact, that her baggage had weighed thirty-seven pounds more than the sixty-six-pound limit for free luggage and that she had thus been compelled to pay an extra twenty-seven dollars in overweight charges. An airline ticket agent recalled suggesting to Mrs. King that she might save some of the money by removing part of her belongings from the suitcase.

Mrs. King reacted to the suggestion by turning to her twenty-three-year-old son, John Gilbert Graham, who had accompanied her to the airport, and asking, "Do you think I'll need all this?"

Graham replied, "Yes, mother. I'm sure you will need it."

Thus, after Mrs. King had paid the overweight charges, her suitcase was loaded into the No. 4 baggage compartment. That suitcase was the only piece of baggage that could not be accounted for after the crash. Although other luggage was shattered, identifiable portions of each suitcase except Mrs. King's were found. The investigators theorized that if the bomb had been inside her suitcase, it might well have been blown to bits.

Their suspicions were heightened when they discovered that her son, Graham, had a criminal record. Four years earlier, while working for a Denver manufacturing firm, he had stolen, forged, and cashed $4,200 worth of the company's checks. He had then fled to Lubbock, Texas, where he had been arrested on bootlegging charges after crashing his car through a police roadblock while officers were shooting at him. Graham served two months in jail for the Texas offenses, then was sent back to Denver to face the forgery charges. But he was released on probation when his mother agreed to repay the money he had received through passing the forged checks.

Graham had then gone to work as manager of a Denver drive-in restaurant owned by his mother. At one point, the investigators were told, Graham had deliberately stalled his pickup truck on a railroad track and left it to be hit by a train in a plot to collect a fraudulent insurance claim. They were also told of a suspicious fire at the drive-in restaurant that resulted in payment of additional insurance benefits.

One of Graham's neighbors reported that Graham had once told him, "I'd do anything for money."

Checking further on Graham, the investigators discovered he had bought three flight-insurance policies on his mother's life at the Denver airport shortly before she boarded Flight 629. On the largest policy, for $37,500, he had written in his own name as the person to be paid in case his mother died in a plane crash. On the two others, for $6,250 each, he had written in the names of two relatives. In view of the reports that Graham had previously been involved in insurance frauds, the investigators naturally grew suspicious that he might have planted the bomb in his mother's suitcase in an attempt to collect on her life insurance.

When they first questioned Graham, he insisted that he had nothing to do with packing his mother's suitcase—that she had done all the packing herself. But interviews with other witnesses produced apparent cracks in that story. Graham's wife, Gloria, told investigators that her husband had gone to the basement of their home with a gift-wrapped package shortly before they drove Mrs. King to the airport. Mrs. Graham said she thought the package contained a set of tools her husband had bought for his mother to use in her favorite hobby, making jewelry from sea shells.

The investigators questioned Graham again, asking him about the tool kit. This time he said he had bought such a kit and secretly slipped it into his mother's suitcase. He claimed two friends had been present when he bought the kit. But when the friends were questioned, they could recall no such purchase.

Graham was told about this discrepancy and other apparent contradictions in his story. He was also told of the evidence that a dynamite explosion had caused the plane crash. "Jack, we have gone over what you told us," one of the investigators said. "You blew up that plane to kill your mother, didn't you?"

"No, I didn't," Graham insisted.

"Then you don't mind if we search your home?"

"No, I don't mind."

While the investigators continued questioning Graham at a government office, his home was searched. Found in one of his shirt pockets was a small coil of wire of the kind used to detonate dynamite. When Graham was confronted with the wire, he could give no explanation for its presence in his home.

Finally, he asked, "Can I have a glass of water?" When he was given the water, he drank almost all of it in one gulp and then said, "Okay, where do you want me to start?"

Graham gave a full confession. He said he and his mother had been arguing for months because their restaurant had been losing money. Finally he came up with the idea of trying to sabotage her plane and collect on her life insurance. He described how he had put together a bomb consisting of twenty-five sticks of dynamite, a timing device, two electric primer caps, and a dry-cell battery. He said he had made room for the bomb in his mother's suitcase by secretly taking out some of her clothing and other belongings.

Among those to whom Graham made the confession was James Peyton, who had commanded an Air Force bomber group during World War II before becoming a CAB investigator. Graham told Peyton he had never heard of the CAB before sabotaging the airliner, but that even the CAB would not have been able to solve the bombing if the plane had not taken off late from Denver. If it had taken off on time, Graham said, the bomb would have exploded while the airliner was over rugged mountains and the CAB would have had trouble recovering the wreckage. Peyton looked at Graham and shook his head. "Son, it wouldn't have made any difference," he said.

After signing a written confession, Graham was initially arrested on federal sabotage charges. He was later turned over to Colorado authorities, who charged him with murder. At his murder trial, Graham at first pleaded not guilty by reason of insanity but later abandoned that defense. A jury found him guilty, and Colorado district judge Edward Keating imposed the death sentence.

On January 12, 1957, after exhausting all his appeals, John Gilbert Graham was executed in the gas chamber at Colorado's Canon City Prison. Despite the severity of his punishment, Graham would not be the last person to try to sabotage an American airliner.

Although his case prompted widespread attempts to devise means of protecting aircraft against hidden bombs, these efforts met with only partial success. No foolproof system was ever discovered.

During the next two decades there were more than a dozen cases in which bombs were planted aboard airliners. Because of tighter security measures, very few actual explosions occurred, and there were only scattered casualties—a marked improvement over previous years. Still, no method could be devised for providing absolute guarantees against sabotage. The problem was compounded by the widespread increase in incidents of terrorism, some of them directed at airliners and air terminals. In January 1976, for example, a bomb planted in a locker at La Guardia Airport in New York City killed eleven persons, and injured scores more.

The problems inherent in trying to discover who is responsible for acts of sabotage—much less prevent them—

were underscored three years after John Graham's execution, when the CAB Bureau of Safety was confronted with an even more complex case than the Colorado mystery.

On the night of January 5, 1960, there were 108 passengers waiting to board a National Airlines flight from New York to Miami. Their Boeing 707 was scheduled to leave at 9:15, but the passengers were told there would be a delay. A crack had been found in the jetliner's windshield, and substitute aircraft would have to be used.

National did not have a sufficiently large substitute airliner available to accommodate all the passengers, so a decision was made to divide them into two groups and fly them to Miami on separate planes. One group would leave at 11:25 aboard a turboprop Electra; the other would leave at 11:51 on an older-model, slower, piston-driven DC-6B. It was to be a first-come, first-served arrangement. Most of the passengers scurried to get in line for the Electra (despite the fact that Electra wing problems had not yet been solved), since the turboprop plane would arrive in Miami much earlier than the DC-6B.

But one passenger who did not seem to hurry was a thirty-two-year-old lawyer named Julian Andrew Frank, who maintained an office in New York and lived in a luxurious home in Westport, Connecticut. Frank was being seen off at the airport by his wife, Janet, a photographer's model whose picture had appeared on many magazine covers. He told her that there was no sense in waiting until his delayed departure, and that she should go home. Frank then walked slowly to the gate where passengers were lining up for the Electra. Despite taking his time, he arrived while there was still a seat left on the Electra.

But then he discovered someone else wanted that seat. Murray and Elizabeth Edwards of New York hoped to fly

on the same plane, but there was room on the Electra for
only one of them. Frank, saying he did not care when he
reached Miami, gave up his place in line to permit Mr. and
Mrs. Edwards to fly together. He then walked to the line of
overflow passengers waiting to board the DC-6B. In one
hand he carried an attaché case; in the other, a blue canvas
airline zipper bag.

The DC-6B, carrying twenty-eight passengers and a
crew of five, took off at 11:52—a minute behind its delayed
schedule. In command was National captain Dale H.
Southard, forty-six, of Miami. The plane rumbled down a
runway and rose slowly into the night. There was a soupy
fog; light rain was falling. But Southard and his crew had
smooth flying for two hours and thirty-nine minutes.

At 2:31 A.M. on January 6, right on schedule, Southard
radioed the airport tower at Wilmington, North Carolina, to
say all was well and that he was about to begin a long
stretch of the flight over the Atlantic toward Florida.

Six minutes later, the early-morning stillness was suddenly shattered by an ear-piercing boom. An explosion had
taken place aboard the airliner, blowing an eight-by-six-foot
hole in the right side of the fuselage. As air rushed from
the pressurized cabin, the plane started disintegrating.
Rocked by buffeting vibrations, it began wobbling in the
manner of a swift-flying quail wounded by a shotgun blast.
Southard and his copilot, R. L. Hentzell, somehow managed to make a descending 120-degree turn to the right and
head back inland. But they were swiftly losing altitude.

After eight minutes, during which they covered twenty
miles, their time played out. The front of the airliner nosed
over, then pounded into the earth with a terrifying boom on
a tobacco farm near Bolivia, North Carolina.

The owner of the farm, Richard Randolph, was awakened by the sound of the plane rumbling low over the

tobacco fields. Then he heard what sounded like two explosions. He looked out into the rain, saw some flames, and considered going out. But when the flames faded, he returned to bed. Thus the wreckage was not discovered until 6:30 A.M., when Randolph's fourteen-year-old son, MacArthur, went out to feed some hogs. He called his father, who determined that nobody had survived the crash and then drove a mile and a half to the nearest phone to notify police.

Meanwhile, the detectives of the sky had been mobilized for an investigation of a possible crash. When Captain Southard and his crew had failed to make their scheduled radio position reports after the one to the Wilmington airport, FAA flight controllers had tried repeatedly to reach the plane. But their radio messages had produced no response, and the detectives of the sky were notified.

Investigators were ordered to proceed immediately to the Wilmington area. By the time they arrived, the wreckage had been spotted. North Carolina state police had begun removing bodies from the area and were awaiting further instructions from the aviation-safety investigators. Heading the investigation for the detectives of the sky was David Thompson, who had been a Navy pilot before joining the CAB Bureau of Safety. Shortly after his arrival, he instructed the state police to tighten security around the crash area to prevent souvenir hunters from taking pieces of the wreckage—a frequent problem at the sites of aircraft accidents.

Thompson then called the nearest military headquarters, the U.S. Marine Corps base at Cherry Point, North Carolina, and arranged to borrow several helicopters for the investigation. His purpose was to try to determine from the air whether all the DC-6B wreckage was in one area. From the helicopters, the investigators discovered that two large pieces of fuselage skin and three passenger seats had landed at Kure Beach on the edge of the Atlantic—a full eighteen miles from the main wreckage. That discovery made it evident that the plane had begun to come apart in the air quite a while before the main section crashed into the tobacco field.

By nightfall, the bodies of thirty-two of the thirty-four persons aboard the plane had been found. The exceptions were attorney Julian Frank and a Cuban banking official named Carlos Ramos. It was not until three days later that Frank's body was discovered, and not until nine days later that Ramos's was found.

The position and condition of Frank's body attracted particular interest from the investigators. It had been found partly submerged in a coastal marsh on the west bank of the Cape Fear River, twenty miles from the main wreckage. The body was mutilated in a manner different from any of the other victims. One leg was cut off above the knee and the other above the ankle. The ends of both legs had been shredded in a way similar to wounds inflicted by land-mine explosions. There was a large hole above Frank's heart. An imprint of the fabric pattern of an airliner seat was found on his hips. Tiny bits of steel, brass, wire, wood, and blue fabric were embedded in his skin. The blue fabric matched that of the canvas airline zipper bag Frank was known to have carried aboard the plane. His body showed slight traces of burns.

In an attempt to determine what had caused the plane to come apart in the air, David Thompson and his fellow investigators began the fantastically complex process of reconstructing a mock-up of the DC-6B. The 15,000 pieces of wreckage were transported to a large hangar at the Wilmington airport, where they were painstakingly identified and hung in place on a chicken-wire model of the airliner fuselage. Construction of the mock-up quickly dis-

This mock-up of the National Airlines plane that crashed near Bolivia, North Carolina, was constructed out of 15,000 pieces of wreckage. It helped investigators pinpoint the location of the explosion that caused the fatal crash.

closed that a large hole had been blown open in the right side of the fuselage. The two pieces of fuselage skin found eighteen miles from the main wreckage had come from that section of the plane, as had the three passenger seats discovered with them. Airline records of the passengers seating arrangements showed that Julian Frank had occupied one of those three seats. That evidence, plus the dis-

covery of Frank's body twenty miles from the main wreckage, convinced the investigators that Frank had been
blown from the plane along with the three seats at the time
the fuselage broke open.

But what had caused it to break open in the first place?
Thompson concluded there were four possibilities. The
first was an airborne collision. The second was explosive
decompression of the pressurized cabin, caused by a propeller blade coming loose and slashing the fuselage. The
third was explosive decompression cause by metal fatigue.
The fourth was an explosive force from inside the cabin
caused by something unknown—possibly a bomb.

One by one, each of the first three possibilites was elimi-
nated by methodical investigation. The investigative team's
operations group made a careful check of all planes in the
area at the time of the accident in an attempt to determine
whether there could have been a collision. Members of the
group also checked to see whether any military aircraft or
ground stations could have fired missiles about that time.
All the findings were negative.

Meanwhile, other investigators determined that a propeller blade could not have slashed the fuselage in this case.
All the propeller blades were found intact, buried in the
earth near the engines at the wreckage site.

The investigative team's structures group reported that
the hole in the fuselage was too large to have been caused
by explosive decompression resulting from metal fatigue.
Corrective construction of airliner fuselages following previous cases of explosive decompression had developed a
cross-webbed type of fuselage structure, which was used
in the DC-6B and would have prevented such a large break
in the cabin wall.

Thus the only possibility remaining was an explosion inside the cabin. Further investigation disclosed that no fuel

lines or other potentially explosive portions of the airliner were near where the gaping hole had been blown in the fuselage. The process of elimination led the investigators to conclude that a bomb must have been planted aboard the plane.

But by whom? And why?

A possible answer to these questions was provided by a mysterious occurrence in New York. One day, shortly after the discovery of Julian Frank's body, a short, graying man in a brown suit, tan coat, and brown hat walked into the lobby of Idlewild Airport (later renamed John F. Kennedy International Airport). The man beckoned for the attention of J. F. Reilly, Jr., the shift station manager for National Airlines.

"I have some information on that flight the other night," he told Reilly. "Julian Frank was one of the passengers. I happen to know that, within the past few months, he took out $500,000 worth of insurance at one time and then added another $200,000. He's been in trouble the last few months. I can't say Frank sabotaged the plane, but he might have. I feel sorry for his wife; she's a wonderful person."

Reilly, who had begun scribbling notes furiously on a pad, looked up to ask a question. But the man had wheeled around and started to walk swiftly away. Reilly called after him, then tried to get an airport police officer to stop him. By that time, however, the man had disappeared into a crowd. His identity was never learned.

Despite the anonymous nature of the tip, an exhaustive investigation into Frank's background was begun. The investigation revealed that Frank's life was, indeed, heavily insured. At the time of his death, he held $1 million worth of insurance policies—with his widow named as the beneficiary.

The son of a former deputy New York City police commissioner, Frank had been a federal prosecutor before entering private law practice. But the investigation revealed that Frank had become involved in a variety of illegal activities in the months before his death. For one thing, he had turned into a confidence man. His pet swindle worked this way: he would accept "finder's fees" from businessmen on the promise that he would get investors to lend them money. After taking the fees, he would fail to deliver the promised loans, but keep the money advanced to him. When he died, Frank was under investigation by the FBI, the Manhattan district attorney's office, and the New York Bar Association for such frauds. He had also been accused by a client of embezzling the $20,000 proceeds of a Manhattan building sale. Lawsuits were pending against him in various parts of the country.

There was also evidence that Frank had become deeply involved with Mafia racketeers. One highly respected New York lawyer who knew Frank and his wife well said Frank had made a trip to Las Vegas about a month before his death and met there with members of the underworld. "I know for a fact that Julian was investing underworld money," the lawyer said. "He told me he was, but he never said who the racketeers were."

Another attorney gave a similar account. He represented Arizona real estate developers who had accused Frank of pulling the "finder's fee" racket on them. After investigating Frank's business affairs, the lawyer concluded that Frank was a swindler. "I got in touch with Frank," the lawyer said. "I told him he was involved in a scheme to defraud and that I was going to the FBI. I said, 'You're using out-of-town money. Where is it coming from?' Frank told me he was getting money (for investment purposes) from people in the underworld. I said, 'You mean you're fronting for them?' He told me, 'What difference does it make? I'm representing them.' He wouldn't identify the underworld people, but he said some of them were from Las Vegas."

Investigators were told that Frank's dealings with the underworld involved secret investments in Boston, Chicago, Phoenix, Las Vegas, and South America. Many of these investments had reportedly gone sour, and there were estimates that Frank had piled up debts totaling almost $2 million within a few months of his death.

At the same time as the investigation of Frank's background was being conducted, the detectives of the sky were pressing ahead with their inquiry into the plane crash itself. In time, laboratory tests produced evidence of nitrate residues—such as those caused by a dynamite explosion—in pieces of the wreckage. Other tests showed the presence of manganese dioxide, indicating that a dry-cell battery might have been used as part of the bomb suspected of blowing the hole in the airliner. Lastly, the investigators made a belated discovery that seemed to cinch the case for the bomb theory. Several weeks after the crash, the investigators found a piece of Julian Frank's amputated leg bone. Embedded in the bone was a piece of an alarm clock.

The conclusion was inescapable. A time bomb—consisting of dynamite, a dry-cell battery, and an alarm clock—had exploded aboard the airliner. The investigators deduced, from the fact that the imprint of the fabric pattern of the airliner seat had been left on Frank's hips, that the bomb had exploded directly under his seat. Other evidence convinced them that the bomb had been inside the zipper bag Frank had carried aboard the plane.

Based on their investigation, the CAB reported on the probable cause of the crash:

It is the board's conclusion that the flight proceeded in a

normal manner without operational difficulty, mechani-
cal failure or malfunction until shortly after passing . . .
a short distance south of Wilmington, North Carolina. A
dynamite charge was exploded, initiated by means of a
dry-cell battery within the passenger cabin and at a point
beneath the extreme right of seat row number seven. Mr.
Julian A. Frank was in close proximity to the dynamite
charge. The dynamite explosion severely impaired the
structural integrity of the aircraft and . . . it experienced
in-flight disintegration and crashed one and a half miles
northwest of Bolivia, North Carolina.

The board deliberately refrained from drawing any conclusion on whether Frank had committed suicide or been
the victim of a murder plot. Arguments could be found for
either possibility, and an investigation continued to try
to determine the truth. Those who favored the suicide
theory pointed to Frank's heavy debts and legal troubles.
They argued that, given those circumstances, it was logical
to assume Frank might have been despondent and killed
himself in at attempt to provide his wife and children with
the financial security available from his $1 million worth
of insurance policies.

Those who leaned toward the theory that Frank had been
murdered pointed out that he had made many enemies
through his illegal ventures and that he had been associating
with racketeers to whom violence was a way of life. Moreover, they argued that some of Frank's actions in the period
shortly before his death were inconsistent with those of a
man bent on suicide. For one thing, before departing on
his ill-fated flight, he had left unsigned an application for
still another insurance policy that would have given his wife
an additional $200,000 worth of death benefits. If he had
planned to kill himself as part of an insurance plot, why

would he have neglected to provide that additional coverage? For another thing, those who favored the murder theory argued, Frank had rejected a double-indemnity provision on some of his insurance—which would have given his widow double benefits in case of an accidental death. If he had planned to disguise a suicide as an accident, why would he have turned down such double benefits? In addition, Frank had bought a round-trip ticket to Florida and planned a trip to Argentina for the week after his trip aboard the doomed airliner. Those did not seen, on the surface at least, to be the acts of an intended suicide victim. Lastly, questions were raised about why he would have used a time bomb. A manually tripped bomb would have been more reliable.

While the various theories were being explored, a new development arose that seemed to provide a possible connection between the Frank case and another airline disaster under investigation by the detectives of the sky. The second crash had taken place on November 16, 1959, about seven weeks before the sabotaging of the plane over North Carolina.

It involved a National Airlines DC-7B that crashed shortly before 1 A.M. in the Gulf of Mexico en route from Tampa, Florida, to New Orleans. Most of the wreckage sank, and all forty-two persons aboard were killed. The few bits of wreckage found floating in the water provided the investigators few clues. Only one eyewitness to the crash could be found, a Coast Guardsman who had been manning a lookout tower near Pilottown, Louisiana, about thirty miles west of the spot where the plane plunged into the Gulf. He reported seeing an unusual light in the sky about the time of the crash.

The Coast Guardsman's account indicated that the airliner could have caught fire or exploded in the air. But the lack of physical evidence resulting from the sinking of most of the wreckage made it impossible for the investigators to draw any firm conclusions about the probable cause of the crash.

Then they discovered mysterious circumstances surrounding one of the passengers on the doomed flight and received information indicating a possible link between the Gulf crash and the bombing of the airliner over North Carolina. Investigation by the FBI and CAB indicated that a notorious character named Robert Vernon Spears with a criminal record spanning forty-three years had persuaded an ex-convict friend—perhaps by hypnosis—to take his place as a passenger on the plane that had crashed in the Gulf. The friend, William Allen Taylor of Tampa, was killed while traveling under Spears's name. He was carrying $100,000 worth of flight insurance, under Spear's name, at the time of his death.

Spears was captured in Phoenix, Arizona, on January 20, 1960. Investigators found a large supply of dynamite in his possession. He later admitted that he had gotten an accomplice to make a bomb for him—supposedly for use against a witness in a criminal case pending against him— and that Taylor might have carried the bomb aboard the airliner downed in the Gulf. Meanwhile, the investigators were told of a connection between Spears and Julian Frank. First, Donald Loomis, a codefendant of Spears in a criminal case in Los Angeles, said Spears had told him at the time of their arrest in that case that he was going to call his lawyer in New York, Julian Frank. Later, it was learned that Frank and Spears had bought insurance from the same underwriter. In addition, evidence was developed that the two men had been doing business with some of the same underworld figures.

Investigators began checking the possibility that a sabotage-murder ring might have been responsible for placing bombs aboard the planes involved in the North Carolina and Gulf crashes. But they were never able to come up with conclusive evidence. Robert Spears was given a five-year prison sentence on charges of stealing a car belonging to William Taylor and driving it across state lines after Taylor's death. The cause of the crash in the Gulf remained officially undetermined—one of the few cases in which the detectives of the sky were forced to mark an accident as unsolved.

There were further developments, however, in the Julian Frank case. The insurance companies that issued the $1 million worth of life insurance to Frank refused to pay off on the policies, claiming Frank had committed suicide and thus made his widow ineligible to collect. Mrs. Frank sued the companies to force them to pay. Her attorney, Morgan P. Ames, contended Frank had been murdered.

At pretrail hearings in the case, Ames tried to establish that Frank's connections with racketeers might have provided a motive for murder. One witness in the hearings, an investor who had done business with .Frank, testified that Frank "indicated to me and to numerous other people" that he was using underworld money. His testimony was corroborated by other men who had done business with Frank. They said Frank had told them of investing money provided by Augie Pisano and fellow racketeers. Pisano was a Mafia leader who had been shot to death in New York on September 25, 1959.

In the end, before the lawsuit over the insurance policies could reach the stage of a full-scale trial, the insurance companies and Mrs. Frank reached an out-of-court settlement. The companies agreed to pay her a substantial part of the money she was seeking, but the exact amount was never made public. Thus the issue of whether Frank had committed suicide or been murdered was left open for speculation, but murder seemed the stronger possibility.

Either way, the sabotage aboard the plane in North Carolina was the twelfth known case in which a bomb exploded on an airliner during a period of little more than ten years.

Following the Frank case investigation, there was a renewed public clamor for improved safeguards to prevent future bombings. Various measures were suggested.

Some people wanted all cargo and baggage placed aboard planes—whether checked in the cargo compartments or hand-carried by passengers—manually searched by security personnel. But the airlines said such a system would be too time-consuming and costly to become practical. Others advocated using devices such as X-ray machines to check baggage for bombs. But such machines were unable to tell a bomb from many harmless items that might be inside the luggage. Still others suggested that insurance companies supply the airlines with names of all individuals who bought large life-insurance policies, so their baggage could be searched whenever they made air trips. But aviation-security experts vetoed the idea as unworkable.

There seemed no means of guaranteeing that a bomb could not be planted aboard an airliner. Several years after the debate over greater antisabotage protection, a wave of airplane hijackings spurred the government to require the airlines to begin inspecting all carry-on luggage taken aboard planes by passengers. The idea was to detect weapons that might be used in attempted hijackings. But this system does not provide for searches of baggage loaded in airliners' cargo compartments. As a result, it is still possible for a saboteur to smuggle a bomb aboard a plane inside a suitcase destined for the cargo section.

The consensus of experts is that the best means of preventing future bombings lies in the skillful investigation of those sabotage cases that do occur and the severe punishment of the persons responsible. It is the hope of these experts that would-be saboteurs will be deterred by the probability that their crimes will be discovered through the scientific detection techniques of the air-safety investigators.

As ever larger numbers of planes take to the skies, the danger of midair collisions becomes increasingly acute. The skies are not limitless; they can become jammed in the same manner as highways. And unless adequate means are used to control the air traffic, disastrous consequences can result.

On occasion, it has taken a tragic midair collision—followed by exhaustive investigation and corrective recommendations from the detectives of the sky—to bring about needed reforms in the nation's air traffic control system. Such was the case, for instance, with an accident that was at the time the worst disaster in commercial aviation history. It took place on June 30, 1956, above the majestic scenery of Arizona's Grand Canyon, and made it painfully clear that more personnel and equipment were needed in FAA ground-control operations.

At 9:01 A.M., Trans World Airlines Flight 2 a Lockheed Constellation—took off from Los Angeles International Airport on its regularly scheduled run to Kansas City, Missouri. In command was TWA captain Jack Gandy, who had been with the airline for seventeen years and had made 177 previous flights on the Los Angeles–Kansas City route. There were five other crew members and sixty-four passengers aboard.

Captain Gandy had filed a flight plan calling for him to fly on instruments at an altitude of 19,000 feet. For part of the flight he would be following a theoretical corridor in the sky designated as Green Airway Five. Only some sections of the sky were divided into such airways. Planes flying within them were under the direct control of air-traffic controllers on the ground. But the old Civil Aeronautics Authority (CAA) did not have sufficient personnel or equipment to track all aircraft in the sky. Thus those flying outside the designated airways operated under so-called see-and-be-seen rules requiring their crews to depend on the naked eye for evading other aircraft. A short time after takeoff, Captain Gandy requested permission by radio to make a slight change in his route to avoid turbulent weather. The change, which took the TWA plane onto another airway, was approved by a CAA controller on the ground.

Three minutes after Gandy's departure from the Los Angeles airport, United Air Lines Flight 718—a Douglas Aircraft DC-7—took off from there on a scheduled flight to Chicago. In command of the United plane was Captain Robert Shirley, another veteran pilot who had logged more than 16,000 hours in the air. Also aboard were four other crew members and fifty-three passengers.

Captain Shirley, like Captain Gandy, would be following Green Airway Five for part of his trip. But his flight plan called for him to maintain an altitude of 21,000 feet—2,000 feet higher than Gandy's plane.

At 9:21, experiencing continued air turbulence, Gandy asked for permission to try to climb above the weather by increasing his altitude to 21,000 feet. The request was initially sent to TWA's central radio base, which passed it on to the CAA traffic-control center in Los Angeles. A Los Angeles controller then relayed it to another CAA controller in Salt Lake City. "How does it look?" the Los Angeles controller in charge of the flight asked. "You have

United [Flight] 718 crossing his altitude—in his way at 21,000 [feet]."

"Yes," the Salt Lake City controller replied. "Their courses cross and they are right together."

The Los Angeles controller, in an attempt to avoid putting the two airliners on a possible collision course, denied permission for Gandy's plane to rise to 21,000 feet. Gandy then made an alternate request. He asked permission to fly "1,000 on top"—meaning 1,000 feet above the clouds in which he was experiencing the turbulence. That request was granted by the Los Angeles controller, who was not aware of the clouds' precise altitudes. At the same time, the controller instructed the TWA radio base to advise Gandy that United Flight 718 would be flying in the same vicinity. Gandy acknowledged receiving the message. In climbing above the clouds, Gandy would be flying under the rules that placed responsibility on him to see and be seen. Because the CAA controllers were busy handling other flights, no message was sent to Captain Shirley in United Flight 718 to keep an eye out for Gandy's plane.

By the time Gandy had climbed 1,000 feet above the clouds, his altitude was 21,000 feet—precisely the height the controllers had wanted him to avoid. The controllers had not stopped to consider that "1,000 on top" might be equivalent to 21,000 feet. At 9:58 A.M., Captain Shirley radioed CAA controllers that he was passing over Needles, Arizona, at 21,000 feet and that he estimated he would fly over the Grand Canyon and reach the Painted Desert at 10:31. A minute later, Captain Gandy radioed that he had passed over Lake Mojave and was also estimating he would reach the Painted Desert at 10:31.

At that point, the two airliners were about fifty miles apart. Both were then flying outside designated airways,

so they were not under the direct supervision of CAA
ground controllers. But the controllers had information in
their possession that both planes expected to reach the
Painted Desert at identical altitudes at the same time. It
seemed logical that this information should have triggered
some alarm bell in the controllers' minds, prompting them
to radio a warning to the converging planes. The controllers were busy with other flights, however, and flashed no
such warning.

At 10:31 the controllers in Salt Lake City picked up a
desperate radio message from Captain Shirley's plane. Shirley's copilot, Robert Harms, was shouting, "Salt Lake. [This
is] United 718. We're going in [to the ground]!" In the
background, someone else could be heard yelling, "Up!
Up!"

That was the last message heard from either plane. At
21,000 feet above the Painted Desert, the two airliners collided. The United DC-7 had been flying slightly behind
and to the right of the TWA Constellation. For some reason, the crewmen of each plane apparently failed to see
the other aircraft until too late. Suddenly they were upon
each other. The left wing tip of Captain Shirley's DC-7
crashed into the center fin of the Constellation's triple tail.
Although both pilots evidently tried to maneuver their
planes apart, the full left wing of the DC-7 then scraped
along the top of the Constellation's fuselage. The DC-7's
propeller blades cut into the Constellation, which immediately began plunging toward the ground. Apparently the
DC-7 was able to stay aloft for a few seconds—but then it,
too, dived into the canyon.

Both planes crashed into the earth with terrifying force
and caught fire. All 128 persons aboard the two planes
were killed—a larger death toll than in any previous com-
mercial-aviation accident.

CAA controllers had no way of knowing at first that there had been a collision. All they knew was that the United plane had seemed to be in some sort of trouble. Repeated messages were radioed to both planes. But, of course, there was no response. The detectives of the sky were notified that one or both aircraft might have been involved in accidents, and investigators immediately began making their way to the Grand Canyon.

Meanwhile, two brothers named Palen and Henry Hudgin, who ran a sight-seeing flight service in the Grand Canyon, noticed some smoke in the Painted Desert area. After hearing that there might have been a crash, the brothers flew over the area in their light plane and spotted the remains of the Constellation's triple tail. Air Force helicopters carrying doctors and rescue workers, then flew to the scene in the hope that there were survivors. But they found only the bodies of the victims and the burned, mangled wreckage of the two aircraft.

The investigators from the CAB Bureau of Safety, headed by Jack Parshall and William Andrews, began their work without being able to assume there had been a collision. Wreckage of the two planes had fallen about a mile apart. It was at least conceivable that there had been separate accidents causing the two aircraft to crash in close proximity.

But then the investigators found a piece of the TWA Constellation wreckage bearing smudges of blue paint. The TWA plane had been painted red and white, so the smudges obviously did not belong there. But the United DC-7 had been painted blue, and scientific analysis showed that the smudges on the Constellation matched the paint from the other plane. This was the first piece of solid evidence that the two aircraft had collided.

The investigators found some pieces of wreckage sufficiently intact to provide important clues to how the collision had occurred. They discovered, for example, three propeller cuts in the rear of the Constellation made by the DC-7. Paint marks at the edge of one cut matched the paint on the DC-7's propellers. Eventually, other sections of both planes provided evidence of damage that could have been made only by a midair collision.

Through painstaking analysis of the wreckage, information of the two planes' flight paths, weather data, and testimony from several persons who said they had caught at least partial glimpses of the collision from the ground, the investigators were able to reconstruct the details of the accident. They determined, among other things, the probable angle at which the airliners had collided, their air speeds, and their altitudes. Other airliners identical to those involved in the accident were test-flown over the collision course. These flights helped produce evidence indicating that the pilots of the ill-fated planes could have had only a few seconds to spot each other and try to take evasive action. Additional evidence indicated that the crews of the downed planes might have been involved in maneuvers designed to give their passengers scenic views of the Grand Canyon during the critical period preceding the collision.

Extensive hearings on the probable cause of the accident were conducted under the direction of CAB Bureau of Safety hearing officer Thomas K. McDill. Assisting him in taking testimony at the hearings were Philip N. Goldstein, investigator in charge of the Bureau of Safety's office in Santa Monica, California; Leon Tanguay, an associate director of the bureau; and Martyn Clarke, a design engineer with the bureau. After considering the evidence produced at the hearings, the full Civil Aeronautics Board issued a report spelling out in detail how the collision had occurred.

The report concluded:

The board determines that the probable cause of this midair collision was that the pilots did not see each other in time to avoid the collision. It is not possible to determine why the pilots did not see each other, but the evidence suggests that it resulted from any one or a combination of the following factors: Intervening clouds reducing the time for visual separation [of the planes]; visual limitations due to cockpit visibility; preoccupation with normal cockpit duties; preoccupation with matters unrelated to cockpit duties, such as attemping to provide the passengers with a more scenic view of the Grand Canyon area; physiological limits to human vision, reducing the time opportunity to see and avoid the other aircraft; or insufficiency of en-route air-traffic advisory information due to inadequacy of facilities and lack of personnel in air-traffic control.

In an attempt to minimize the danger of future collisions, the CAB made several recommendations for expanding and improving the nation's air-traffic control system. Amid a broad general clamor for tighter safety standards prompted by the heavy loss of life in the Grand Canyon collision, Congress agreed to increase substantially the amount of money appropriated for the personnel and equipment needed to operate the system. At the time of the collision, only $16 million a year was being spent on air-traffic control. By the next year the amount had jumped to $75 million. New radar equipment, navigation and communications devices, and other facilities were installed. Additional controllers were hired.

Meanwhile, federal regulations were changed to put more flights under the direct supervision of ground controllers. All civilian and military flights operating at altitudes of 17,000 feet and higher were placed under positive ground control. Jetliners flying at higher speeds and altitudes than piston-driven planes received additional protection under a system that provided for constant radar monitoring of all aircraft operating at altitudes above 24,000 feet.

Still, there was no guarantee against midair collisions. In April 1958, an Air Force jet fighter collided with a United Air Lines DC-7 near Las Vegas—killing all forty-nine persons aboard the airliner. A month later, twelve more persons were killed when an Air National Guard jet collided with a Capitol International Airways plane over Brunswick, Maryland.

But these accidents were overshadowed by a disastrous collision over New York City on December 16, 1960. Involved were a United Air Lines DC-8 and a TWA Super Constellation.

The United jetliner, designated Flight 826, took off at 8:10 A.M. from O'Hare Airport in Chicago for New York's Idlewild (now Kennedy) Airport. A crew of seven, headed by Captain R. H. Sawyer, was aboard with seventy-seven passengers, many of them leaving early on Christmas holiday trips. The TWA Constellation, Flight 266, was bound for La Guardia Airport in New York from Municipal Airport in Dayton, Ohio. A piston-driven plane, it flew at slower speeds than the United jet. TWA captain David Wollam, four other crew members, and thirty-nine passengers were aboard the Constellation.

At 10:28 A.M. the TWA plane radioed La Guardia approach controllers that it was circling in a holding pattern 9,000 feet above Linden, New Jersey, awaiting clearance to land. The controllers radioed back that they anticipated no delays, that light snow was falling at La Guardia and visibility there was one mile. A short time later, they instructed the plane to descend to 5,000 feet.

Meanwhile, the United jet was approaching another holding pattern area designated as the Preston Intersection, which was only about five miles from the Linden holding area and was used by planes waiting to land at Idlewild. Captain Sawyer reported his altitude to ground controllers as 14,000 feet. He was given clearance to make a rapid descent to 5,000 feet.

"Look like you'll be able to make Preston at five [5,000 feet]?" a controller asked.

"We'll head it right on down," Sawyer replied. "We'll dump it."

The United DC-8 was traveling at almost 500 miles an hour as it descended. At La Guardia Airport, a controller monitoring a radar device in preparation for giving landing instructions to TWA Flight 266 noticed an unexpected blip representing a plane on his screen south and east of the TWA Constellation.

The controller was not particularly alarmed at first by the blip, figuring the second plane was probably flying at a different altitude from the TWA Constellation. (At the time, the radar equipment in standard use was not three-dimensional. It showed a plane's latitude, longitude, and flight path—but not its altitude.) Nonetheless, the controller radioed Captain Wollam in the Constellation to inform him of the second plane's presence. "Trans World 266, traffic . . . six miles, northeast bound," he warned.

As the controller continued watching his radar screen, however, he grew increasingly concerned. The second blip was traveling at high speed—obviously indicating the plane was a jet—in the direction of TWA Flight 266. "There appears to be jet traffic off your right wing," he radioed Captain Wollam. "Now . . . at one mile from you, northeast bound."

He waited for a response, but heard only the sound of an

open microphone in the TWA plane's cockpit—indicating someone was about to speak. No voice came over the microphone, however, and the controller called the plane several times. Still there was no reply.

At 10:32 A.M. United Flight 826 had been instructed to radio approach controllers at Idlewild Airport for holding and landing instructions. A minute later, Captain Sawyer did so. "Idlewild Approach Control, United 826 approaching Preston at 5,000 [feet]," he said.

"Roger, 826," the controller replied. "And hold at 5,000." He spent the next sixteen seconds giving Sawyer weather and landing information. But, at the end of his message, he did not receive the mandatory acknowledgment of the instructions from Sawyer. The controller tried repeatedly to reach the United jet, but got no response.

Meanwhile, at La Guardia Airport, the radar controller handling TWA Flight 266 recognized something was radically wrong. "I think we have trouble here with a Connie [a Constellation]," he informed the La Guardia control tower. "There's something wrong. He's not moving or anything. He might've got hit by—by another plane." The controller had seen two blips on his screen come together, then seen a partial blip flicker off toward the Flatbush section of Brooklyn.

A La Guardia controller radioed his counterpart at Idlewild, "Is that your traffic at Flatbush?"

"No, it's not our traffic, La Guardia," the Idlewild controller replied.

"Well, now he's—we lost communication with an aircraft and something may be wrong with him."

"Wait a minute, La Guardia," the Idlewild controller said. In the background, someone at Idlewild could be heard asking, "Do you think that might be him? One over

Flatbush?" Then the Idlewild controller said, "It could be ours on approach control, New York."

"Yeah, well what type aircraft is that?" the La Guardia controller asked.

"A United DC-8."

"And what, and what's his altitude?"

"He was last cleared to 5,000."

"Oh, boy, our man was at five, too. We lost one aircraft. I don't know where he's at now."

"We haven't been able to, I haven't identified United yet," the Idlewild controller said.

"Yeah, well, he's going right over our approach course; he's coming up on our outer [radar] marker now," the La Guardia controller replied.

Moments later, the La Guardia controller placed an emergency call to the FAA's control center for New York. (By 1960, the FAA had been established to replace the old CAA.) "This is La Guardia. I think we got an emergency," the controller said. "Nobody declared anything, but who is that jet or fast-moving aircraft that went from Preston towards Flatbush?"

A voice at the control center asked, "From Preston towards Flatbush?"

"Yes. He's at Flatbush right now."

"A fast-moving aircraft going where? Know his destination?"

"I don't know. Now, listen to this! He may have hit one of our aircraft. We're not sure."

"All right, just stand by."

"New York, New York!"

"Go ahead, La Guardia. What do you have?"

"All right, now we got troubles, but we're not sure of it. We lost contact with a TWA—266, I believe his number

Fire fighters, rescue workers, and investigators pick their way through the wreckage of a United Air Lines jet that crashed on a crowded Brooklyn street on December 16, 1960. The crash resulted from a midair collision with a TWA Constellation jetliner.

As a part of the investigation following the midair collision of the TWA and United jetliners, the planes were reconstructed from pieces of the wreckage in a hangar at La Guardia Airport.

is—he was on a collision course with an aircraft, an unknown aircraft heading northeast from Preston towards Flatbush. That aircraft now is a mile outside the La Guardia outer marker heading northeast-bound."

The ground controllers had no way of knowing it for sure at the time, but what had happened 5,000 feet in the air was that the United DC-8 had crashed into the TWA Constellation. The extreme right jet engine of the DC-8 had broken off and lodged in the upper right side of the Constellation's cabin. Carrying the other plane's engine with it, the Constellation plunged to earth on Staten Island in New York City. Meanwhile, the DC-8—even though missing one of its four engines—managed to limp across another eight miles before crashing in a densely populated section of Brooklyn. All 128 persons aboard both planes were killed, as were 6 people crushed by falling debris on the ground in Brooklyn.

Once again, the detectives of the sky began the grim task of trying to determine what had been responsible for a major disaster. Using techniques similar to those followed after the Grand Canyon accident, the investigators carefully traced the paths taken by the two airliners involved in the New York collision. They discovered that the United DC-8 had been far off course at the time it ran into the Constellation.

When the DC-8 had radioed Idlewild approach controllers at 10:33 A.M. that it was "approaching Preston at 5,000 [feet]," the plane had actually flown eleven miles past the Preston Intersection. The investigators found that Captain Sawyer, apparently unaware he had flown past his assigned position, was piloting the jetliner through the buffer zone designed to separate planes waiting to land at Idlewild from those waiting to land at La Guardia. When he continued on that course, his plane eventually collided with the Constellation.

A possible reason for the DC-8 crew's confusion over its position, the investigators discovered, was that one of the plane's radio navigation receivers—used as a direction-finder—was not working as the jet approached New York. The crew had radioed information on the problem to its company headquarters, but this information had not been relayed to the FAA. There was some speculation that, if the FAA controllers had known about the malfunction, they might have taken special precautions in tracking the DC-8's position as it approached New York.

In any event, the CAB determined that "pilot error" was the probable cause of the collision. "United Flight 826 proceeded beyond its clearance limit and the confines of the airspace allocated to the flight by [FAA] Air Traffic Control," the CAB reported. It said the jet's high speed as it approached the Preston Intersection could have been another contributing factor in leading the plane to overshoot its clearance point.

Again, based on the investigation by the detectives of the sky, new remedial steps were ordered to try to avert future collisions. Jets were ordered to fly at slower speeds when approaching areas where the skies were crowded with planes. Additional ground controllers were employed at major air terminals and assigned to concentrate on preventing airliners from straying beyond the limits of their holding patterns. Sophisticated new devices designed to improve aircraft crews' navigation procedures were ordered installed in stages on all airliners—first on jets, then on prop-jets, and finally on piston-driven planes.

Following the adoption of these reforms, there was a marked improvement in the aircraft industry's record in avoiding midair collisions. There is still, of course, no iron-clad guarantee against such collisions. Human errors and equipment malfunctions are always possible.

On October 11, 1974, for example, a New Jersey Air National Guard F-104 fighter plane collided with a small private plane over Saxis, Virginia. Scarcely a month later, there was another collision between an Air Force F-111 fighter and a plane owned by the Montana Power Company near Kingston, Utah. Then, on January 9, 1975, an Air Force transport and a light plane collided over Newport

News, Virginia. And on that same day, a Golden West Airlines plane collided with a light aircraft over Whittier, California. In all, twenty-eight persons were killed in the four crashes.

Although there have been few major midair collisions involving commercial airliners in recent years, there have been numerous near-misses. In late 1975 and early 1976 many pilots and ground controllers complained that FAA requirements—particularly those aimed at saving fuel costs for the airlines—resulted in lax safety measures. One controller, in fact, was suspended for three days by the FAA for refusing to abide by regulations that he felt were unsafe.

It is thus obvious that wrinkles remain in the air-traffic control system. Improvements have been made since the Grand Canyon and New York City disasters, but there is still room for more—and the detectives of the sky are pressing for their adoption. (See chapter 8.)

Although there are similarities among air-crash disasters, no two are ever identical. Each presents the detectives of the sky with a new mystery that must be solved. The lessons learned in one investigation may provide the answers to a later riddle, so the National Transportation Safety Board must constantly remain alert for new problems and new means of solving them. Examination of a few recent case histories demonstrates the broad variety of accident causes that must be discovered. In each case, the investigators methodically piled fact upon fact before sat isfying themselves that they had determined the probable cause of the crash.

There was, for example, the crash of a Pan American World Airways cargo jet at Boston's Logan Airport on November 3, 1973. The jet had taken off from New York's Kennedy Airport on a scheduled flight to Frankfurt, West Germany, with a planned stop at Prestwick, Scotland.

Shortly after the plane's departure, the three crew members noticed smoke inside the plane. They assumed it was coming from a minor electrical fire, and radioed ground controllers that they would set down for repairs in Boston, where Pan Am had maintenance facilities. But thirty-five minutes later the jet crashed 262 feet from the end of a runway while trying to land at Boston. The three crew members were killed.

NTSB investigators, checking the wreckage for clues, could find no evidence of electrical problems that would have caused the smoke reported by the crew. Other clues directed their attention to the plane's cargo. The jet had been carrying a seven-ton shipment of chemicals, including nitric and sulfuric acid.

Under FAA regulations, such acids and other hazardous items could be shipped by air only if strict safety requirements were followed in packing them. The NTSB investigators interviewed more than one hundred persons in an attempt to determine whether those requirements had been met in the case of the cargo aboard the plane that had crashed. They found that many rule violations had been committed.

The FAA regulations provided, for example, that a shipper of hazardous materials must "thoroughly instruct employees" on the applicable rules. Yet the young clerk who had supervised packing of the chemical shipment admitted he knew almost nothing about the regulations. He had not even been provided a correct set of instructions by his employer. And he had signed a set of forms certifying that the chemicals had been properly packed even before the packing had been done.

Moreover, the regulations provided that each bottle of nitric acid must be placed in a tightly closed metal container and cushioned on all sides by flame-resistant material such as asbestos. But the nitric acid placed aboard the Pan Am plane was not protected by metal containers and was cushioned with sawdust, which easily catches fire. Sawdust was specifically prohibited by the regulations from use in packing nitric acid.

Beyond all that, the NTSB investigators discovered, loading crews at Kennedy Airport had ignored this-side-up arrows on the crates holding the acid. They had placed the crates on their sides, thus making it likely that acid would leak from one or more of the bottles.

The investigators found that acid had leaked from at least one bottle, starting a fire when it came in contact with the sawdust. Dense smoke then filled the cockpit, temporarily blinding the three crew members and forcing them to put on oxygen masks. Although they were wearing smoke goggles, they were unable to see their instruments. They were also unable to communicate with each other. These factors combined to bring about the fatal crash, the NTSB reported. Other contributing elements, the investigators said, were the improper design of the smoke goggles, which could not fully protect the wearers' eyes; an inadequate smoke-clearance system on the airplane; and inadequate emergency procedures that made the plane virtually impossible to land.

The NTSB report said the FAA regulations for shipment of hazardous materials were inadequate and that enforcement of the existing regulations was lax. On the basis of recommendations made in the report, steps were taken to tighten both the regulations and enforcement policies.

On March 4, 1976, a federal grand jury in New York returned an unprecedented criminal indictment accusing Pan Am, another corporation, and an individual of causing the Boston crash by unlawfully transporting dangerous chemicals. The indictment charged the airline, a moving company named Santini Brothers, Inc., of the Bronx; and one of Santini's employees, William Higgins, with violating FAA regulations on the marking, packing, and transporting of dangerous materials. Justice Department officials said a five-month investigation by the grand jury had revealed that almost a third of the plane's cargo had consisted of dangerous chemicals, weighing close to 5,000 pounds. More than half the chemicals—including the nitric acid—were improperly packed, and almost all of them were improperly marked for air transportation, the officials said.

Higgins was office manager for Santini's facility in Maspeth, Queens, near Kennedy Airport. The indictment said Santini had delivered the materials to Pan Am for shipment by air to Scotland. Pan Am pleaded no contest to the charges in the indictment, the first of its kind returned against an airline. Pan Am could be fined a maximum of $60,000. Santini Brothers and its employee, Higgins, pleaded not guilty and are awaiting trial at this writing. Santini Brothers could be fined $275,000 if convicted; Higgins could be imprisoned for eleven years and fined $11,000 if found guilty.

Another case in which an NTSB investigation indicated that improper loading of cargo might have caused a fatal crash involved an accident near Miami International Airport on December 15, 1973. A Super Constellation owned by the Aircraft Pool Leasing Corporation, carrying a load of Christmas trees bound for Caracas, Venezuela, took off from the Miami airport shortly before midnight. As it rose from the ground, FAA controllers noticed that the plane's nose was pointing toward the sky at an abnormally sharp angle. The plane reached a maximum altitude of only about 120 feet. It then plunged toward the ground and hit high-tension wires and a tree before crashing into several homes and automobiles. The three crew members and six persons on the ground were killed.

The NTSB investigation revealed that no restraining devices had been used to hold in place the 666 bundles of Christmas trees loaded aboard the plane. Nor was there evidence that the cargo was so tightly packed that it could not shift position inside the cargo compartment. Although the weight of the cargo was supposed to be distributed evenly throughout the compartment, the NTSB reported that there were indications of a heavier concentration of Christmas trees toward the rear of the plane than toward the front.

In its report on the crash, the NTSB said such uneven

weight toward the rear of the plane "would explain the abrupt, nose-high" position of the aircraft on takeoff. It said the plane's engines had gone into a near-stall, and that the aircraft was at such a low altitude that the crew was unable to correct the problem before crashing. The report concluded: "Factors which may have contributed to the accident include: (a) improper cargo loading; (b) a rearward movement of unsecured cargo resulting in a shift of the center of gravity aft of the allowable limit; and (c) deficient crew coordination."

On September 11, 1974, an Eastern Airlines DC-9 crashed three miles short of a runway while trying to land at Douglas Municipal Airport near Charlotte, North Carolina. Seventy-two of the eighty-two persons aboard were killed. NTSB detectives of the sky who investigated the crash could find no mechanical troubles responsible for the accident. But they discovered other clues when they retrieved the voice-recorder that had taped conversations in the cockpit during the critical period just before the crash.

The tape revealed that the plane's pilot and copilot were talking about everything from school desegregation and the pardon of former President Richard M. Nixon to Japanese automobiles and Arab oil policies when they should have been concentrating on landing procedures. Excerpts from the taped conversation included the following quotations:

Well, what they're doing is to force all the whites to go to private schools and the public [schools] are going to end up black. That's exactly what's going to happen. . . .

They're going to come out with a law and say, okay, now we're gonna integrate the private schools. Therefore, you white folks are going to have to take all these blacks going to your white schools. . . .

Can't leave well enough alone, can they? . . .

Government's got too big. One out of every sixteen people working for the government. . . .

While such conversation was taking place, the NTSB said, the crew members failed to comply with regulations requiring them to call out the plane's altitude as it descended toward the airport. They also failed to note that the plane was 450 feet below its assigned minimum altitude as it passed a radio checkpoint 5½ miles from the airport, the NTSB reported.

The last seconds of recorded conversation indicated the crewmen were unsure of their position as they tried to land. "All we have to do is find the airport," one of them said.

"Yeah," the other replied. This last word was followed on the tape by the booming sound of the jetliner crashing into the ground.

The NTSB report said the probable cause of the crash was the failure of the crew to keep track of the plane's altitude. It said the conversation on matters having nothing to do with operation of the aircraft had played a definite role in the disaster. As the report put it:

During the descent, until about two minutes and thirty seconds prior to the sound of impact, the flight crew engaged in conversations not pertinent to the operation of the aircraft that were distractive and reflected a casual mood and lax atmosphere, which continued throughout the remainder of the approach and which contributed to the accident. The overall lack of cockpit discipline was manifested in a number of respects where the flight crew failed to adhere to recommended or required procedures.

In a separate statement commenting on both the Charlotte crash and other accidents, the NTSB said it had found numerous examples of pilot carelessness. "Investigations have revealed that crew behavior ranges from the casual acceptance of the flight and environment to flagrant disregard for prescribed procedures and safe operating practices," the statement said. It added that the Charlotte crash "reflects once again serious lapses in expected professional conduct."

The NTSB urged the FAA to take several steps to eliminate such problems. It recommended that the FAA initiate a movement among pilot groups to monitor their own ranks for evidence of substandard flight performance. And it suggested a parallel monitoring program be launched by the airlines. The FAA agreed with the recommendations, and immediately began implementing them.

A different sort of problem confronted the detectives of the sky when they were called upon to investigate the crash of a Western Airlines Boeing 720 jet at Ontario, California, on March 31, 1971. The plane was making a routine training flight over Ontario International Airport at the time of the accident. Five crew members were the only occupants of the plane.

In order for the crew to practice an emergency-landing procedure that might be necessary if an engine failed, one of the plane's four engines had been reduced to idle power. The flight was cleared either to land or to execute a so-called missed approach (that is, come in as if to land, not actually set down, but rise and circle for another attempted landing). When the plane had descended to a point where a decision had to be made on whether to land—about 100 feet above the runway—a missed-approach procedure was begun. The plane started to climb, and the crew retracted the landing gear. Then, as the aircraft continued to climb to 500 feet above the runway, it suddenly rolled to the right. Its nose dropped to a near-vertical downward posi-

tion. The plane went into a dive and crashed about 420
feet from the runway. All five occupants were killed.

The NTSB investigators, after extensive metallurgical
analysis of the wreckage, discovered that an in-flight structural failure had taken place on a support fitting on the
plane's rudder. This failure had resulted in the pilot's loss
of left-rudder control. Without that control, he was unable
to right the plane and the crash followed, the NTSB reported. It attributed the failure of the rudder fitting to "a
combination of the weakening effects of stress-corrosion
cracking" and application of near-maximum pressures on
the fitting during the training flight.

In conducting their investigation, the detectives of the
sky found that both the manufacturer of the plane and
the FAA had known of previous trouble with rudder support fittings on Boeing 720s. At least twice during the two
years before the California crash, Boeing and the FAA had
issued alerts about potential fitting problems to users of the
planes. But the NTSB said these warnings had been inadequate and had not provided for sufficiently frequent inspec-
tions to assure the fittings were sound. It recommended
stricter remedial action, which was taken by the FAA.

It should be obvious at this point that the nation's system for preventing aviation disasters is far from perfect. There is still too much resistance by airlines, manufacturers, and others within the industry to safety recommendations made by the National Transportation Safety Board, the Federal Aviation Administration, and flight-crew unions. There is still too much emphasis placed by the unions on protecting their members' interests at the cost of the passengers' interests. There is still too much bureaucratic red tape—too many delays, for instance, by the FAA in implementing NTSB suggestions.

Yet the picture is not all bleak. Investigations by Congress and the U.S. General Accounting Office have pointed the way toward genuine reforms. The tragic errors of the past have apparently awakened in the FAA, the airlines, and other segments of the industry greater awareness that it is necessary to lean over backward on the side of caution —rather than place greatest emphasis on the dollar cost of safety improvements.

For example, after seventy-five persons were killed in the crash of a Southern Airways DC-9 in 1970 at Huntington, West Virginia, the NTSB urged installation on all large jets of a device designed to warn flight crews that they were flying too low. The device cost only $10,000, but even that moderate cost—when applied to every jet in the sky—represented an investment the airlines were reluctant to make. The FAA did not initially compel them to do so.

The device in question, known as a ground-proximity warning system, is a small, boxlike computer that plugs into existing airplane instruments such as the altimeter, the glide-slope receiver, and the landing-gear controls. Whenever a plane equipped with the device descends too fast, dips beneath its approved glide slope, closes too quickly with the ground, or fails to climb properly on takeoff, a flashing light appears on the instrument panel and a loud recorded voice fills the cockpit, warning, "Whoop, whoop, pull up!" The warning light and sound do not stop until the crew takes corrective action.

After the NTSB made its initial recommendation that such devices be installed, the FAA dragged its feet on implementing the suggestion. It was not until four years later —after ninety-two persons were killed when a TWA jet crashed into a mountain not far from Dulles International Airport outside Washington, D.C., on December 1, 1974— that the FAA ordered the warning systems installed on all commercial jetliners.

Apparently learning from such mistakes, the FAA is currently becoming more aggressive in seeking out safety devices—no matter what the cost. It has, for instance, granted a $527,000 contract to an inventor, George B. Litchford of Northport, New York, to produce experimental models of a device he has built and patented as an aid to preventing midair collisions. The device, called a collision-avoidance system, permits an aircraft to determine the flight path of another plane by intercepting radar signals. Although Litchford's gadget is still in the development stage, the FAA's investment of more than a half-million dollars— with NTSB support—represents a confident expectation that the device will someday be standard equipment aboard airliners. While no such instrument is foolproof, it could help prevent repetitions of the Grand Canyon and New York City collisions.

The emphasis in this book on disasters that have occurred in the past should not be taken as indicating that airline travel is an intrinsically unsafe mode of transportation. Quite the opposite is true.

Lloyd's of London, the authoritative insurance company, calculates that a person is twenty-four times more likely to be killed in a car than in an airliner. Other statistics indicate that a passenger on a scheduled airline flight in the United States has a 99.99992 percent chance of arriving safely at his or her destination. In the last decade, U.S. airline accidents per mile flown have been cut by two-thirds, and fatalities per passenger mile have been reduced by 50 percent. If a person were born on an airliner and flew every day from that time on without ever getting off the plane, statistics indicate that he or she could not expect to be involved in a fatal accident until well past the age of seventy.

Of course, there is always room for further improvement in the aviation-safety record. Such improvement will require close cooperation among the many segments of the industry—including the aircraft manufacturers, the airlines, the employee unions, ground controllers, and others. And, to a large extent, it will likely depend on the continued dedication, perseverance, and technical skill of the National Transportation Safety Board's detectives of the sky.

Acknowledgments

I am deeply indebted to the members and employees of the National Transportation Safety Board for their cooperation. I would like particularly to thank Edward Slattery, the NTSB public-information director, who has long been regarded by writers as the very model of what a government information officer ought to be.

I would also like to express my appreciation to officials and employees of the Federal Aviation Administration, various airlines and aircraft manufacturers, the Air Line Pilots Association, and the Flight Engineers International Association for sharing with me their thoughts on the difficult problems of aviation safety.

To Lynn Sonberg and Dorothy Markinko, my thanks for faith, counsel, and patience.

As always, my wife, Jeanne, and daughters, Pamela and Patricia, merit appreciation for putting up with the rigors of life in a writer's household.

In addition to the published reports of the NTSB, various books provided valuable background information. Some of them are included in the bibliography.

Bibliography

Halacy, D. S., Jr. *America's Major Air Disasters*. New York: Monarch Books, 1961.

Johnson, George. *The Abominable Airlines*. New York: Macmillan, 1964.

Mallan, Lloyd. *Great Air Disasters*. New York: Fawcett, 1962.

Marx, Joseph L. *Crisis in the Skies*. New York: David McKay, 1970.

Ottenberg, Miriam. *The Federal Investigators*. Englewood Cliffs, N.J.: Prentice-Hall, 1962.

Serling, Robert J. *The Probable Cause*. New York: Doubleday, 1960.

Index

About the Author

An award-winning former journalist, Michael Dorman has worked as a reporter for *The New York Times, Newsday,* and *Newsweek.* He is the author of numerous books for both adults and young people on political and social issues, including *Confrontation: Politics and Protest,* and *Under 21: A Young People's Guide to Legal Rights. Detectives of the Sky* is Mr. Dorman's first book to be published by Franklin Watts. The author lives with his family on Long Island, New York.